Life At Levers

Memories of making soaps at Port Sunlight.

David Roberts

An Avid Publication

© William David Roberts 1995
Published by :
Avid Publications
7 Garth Boulevard
Bebington, Wirral
Merseyside L63 5LS.
United Kingdom.
Tel / Fax 0151 645 2047
Copies of this book can be obtained from the
above.

I.S.B.N No.0 9521020 3 X

Edited by William David Roberts
All Rights Reserved

Also published by Avid Publications:

Cammell Laird - the golden years, by David Roberts I.S.B.N 0 9521020 2 1

Life at Lairds - memories of working shipyard men, by David Roberts I.S.B.N 0 9521020 1 3

Cammell Laird - Old ships and Hardships , the story of a shipyard. On Video.

Off the Cuff - policing on Merseyside, by Swasie Turner. I.S.B.N 0 9521020 4 8

<u>Acknowledgements</u>

This book would not exist without those people who agreed to talk about their lives at Levers and I thank them all. Many of them loaned me books, private photographs and letters for possible inclusion in this book and I am thankful for their encouragement.

However, Eric Coates, Fitter Extraordinaire, and something of a historian himself, gave me a great deal of assistance and of his time. I am deeply grateful. Eric is the self appointed Commodore of the Gobi Desert Sailing Club. My thanks Eric, and keep taking the tablets.

Joanne Bird , Pauline Dickson and Jan Purssell for doing the transcribing. Again.

Jan. She knows who she is. For providing the audio transcription machine. My thanks.

Mark Rickards, and Pauline Dickson for proof reading. Again.

El Sluggo, who, as ever, kept me going when I got tired and lacklustre about the whole book.

Denise Roberts. She knows why.

The Sony Corporation, who sold a compact cassette recorder to me some eight years ago. It's still doing the business and has heard many tales of working life. I hope it will hear many more.

Photograph of William Hesketh Lever by permission of I.L.N. Plc

Soap Trust Cartoon reproduced by kind permission of Mirror Group Newspapers.

Cover Photograph: The girls, & some men on just one shift circa 1980. Val Button kneeling, 2nd from right. Irene Mounsey, 1st on left first standing row. Are you there?

'Billy' Lever
1851-1925

The Tale of Spinning Billy

When we get visitors round Port Sunlight Village and they talk about the village I say to them "Have you been to the Art Gallery?"
"Oh yes", they say.
"Have you been down to the Church?"
"No, not yet".

I tell them that the best time to go down to the church is on a cool, quiet summer evening. Look on the left hand side of the church entrance for the little notice which says Founder's Tomb. Billy Lever is dossed down there. If you listen very carefully you'll hear a humming sound like a turbine, as you get closer the whining, humming noise gets a little louder, and a little louder - that's old Billy Lever spinning in his grave because of what they've done to his factory.

I reckon if they wired him up he could keep this village going on electricity.

Richard Godwin- retired Lever employee
Port Sunlight 1995

INTRODUCTION

Levers.

Not the kind of lever that we think of as a simple machine for helping us manoeuvre heavy objects but a place that in the not too distant past employed tens of thousands of people, at a place known as Port Sunlight , on the western side of the River Mersey in the North of Britain. The factory is still there , though employing many thousands of people less. This place has universally become know as 'Levers' after is proprietors' surname. Today it is a part of the huge multinational conglomerate UNILEVER.

In some respects though Levers is a simple machine. A machine that uses the resources of men and women , chemicals and factory processes to produce a simple everyday item that we all use. Soap. Soap for hands and faces , soap for washing clothes and soap for cleaning floors and kitchens.

The founding father of this cleaning Empire was one William Hesketh Lever, known to one and all who worked at Levers factory as 'Billy' Lever , held in high regard by some , less so by others.

Much has already been written about the start of Levers enterprise in soap, from it's humble beginnings in Warrington , just south and east of Liverpool , in 1885 , through his building of the 'model' village of Port Sunlight on the Wirral , started in 1888, and the ultimate amalgamation with the Dutch Margarine - Union in 1930 , forming the mammoth multinational corporation known all over the world as UNILEVER.

Levers at Port Sunlight has long stood in employment folk-lore for fairness, equality of opportunity , good working conditions and reasonable wages. 'They look after you ' is a phrase that persists in this same folk- lore. Levers is often referred to by some observers and some historians as a 'paternalistic ' organisation, in the context of a father figure who looks after your interests.

The danger with this view is that the actual concept of paternalism means something a little different from the images we see in the sanitised histories of Levers , happy smiling faces whistling down the road from their 'model' homes in Port Sunlight , to work in the factory making soap.

The dictionary defines Paternalism as :-
" kind but oppressive rule , benevolent tyranny.", a far cry from the

context of the great benefactor.

The various histories and celebratory publications of this company have carefully avoided any notion that 'Billy ' Lever was anything other than a great philanthropist , in a similar vein as the histories of The British Empires' expansionism into Africa and Asia was presented as "Free Trade" and not what it really was, the strangulation and exploitation of infant economies.

There is no question that the village of Port Sunlight is one of the prettiest in Britain today and that the houses , slowly being brought up to late twentieth century housing standards, but not by the company, are highly desirable properties. Amongst other things, the Lever organisation of today have abdicated that self proclaimed Lever policy of the turn of the century to provide housing for the workforce and are now selling the houses off to the highest bidder on the open market. Port Sunlight could be described as an oasis of existence within an industrialised area.

The rose-coloured version of the Villages creation , of Billy Levers benevolence to his employees in providing them with housing at reasonable rents , pensions ,and recreational facilities (Once upon a time there was a communal outdoor swimming pool), The Lady Lever Art Gallery is still open to the public, as is the bowling green and the Social Clubs, is of course available to anyone who wishes to subscribe. This perspective can be reinforced by pointing to the health care the company provided too , Dental and Ophthalmic care being available to all employees.

Another side of the coin is less well publicised.

Billy Lever was a Capitalist.

Nothing wrong with that at all . He was in the business of making soap to make money. But let's say so. He built his workforces houses in Port Sunlight to indulge himself with the designs and layout of the site and to provide his enterprise with a compliant workforce that , once ensconced in a Lever House , would be less inclined to be critical of any aspect of the organisation.

He bought the land at Port Sunlight , all 56 acres of it, for £11,000, and in the words of his grandson , the present , and probably last Viscount Leverhulme , " he was trying to build a village where people were happy and drawing money on a Friday night wasn't the most important thing in life...... he'd probably be proud of it today , but not too happy about selling off the houses. " [1]

It is commonly said , that he bankrupted many an architect and builder of the period in order to get what he wanted at the price that he wanted, for his model village. As the biggest and richest client around he called the tune , in much the same way as the huge shopping superstores of today have the greatest purchasing power from suppliers.

'Billy ' Lever was the son of a Grocer . A common thread from the contributors to this book is that " Lever's isn't like it used to be " .... "it's all changed now, and not for the better", but then, as we approach the millennium, does anything stay the same ?

The charge is that ' they don't care about the people anymore' .... 'it's all down to the so - called market economy '.......'Horizon 2000 is all they care about now .' If true , it is ironic that some 60 years after his death in 1925 , that another grocers' sibling one Margaret, and her market economy philosophy, should have such a devastating effect upon old 'Billy' Levers legacy .

Horizon 2000 , referred to by some employees as 'Horror- Zone 2000 ' is a new concept embraced by the company and apparantly imposed upon it's workforce , of flexible working and "multi - tasking" for employees , making , in simple terms , each employee his or her own manager , production controller and quality controller. Or, perhaps a euphemism for what is referred to in management circles in the United States as , "More for less" ... " getting more out of the workforce for less costs."

It is perverse in the extreme that this exact philosophy, getting more income for less costs, got William Lever into trouble in 1906 when, due to a sharp rise in the costs of raw materials , he introduced the one pound bar of Sunlight soap that only weighed 15 ounces. This was the subject of a famous cartoon in the Daily Mirror depicting a bloated 'Mr Soap Trust', presumably Lever , and a poor woman complaining that her bar of soap was an ounce short , being treated heavy handedly by the seller. The backdrop of the cartoon showed posters with captions about sackings at 'Port Moonshine' and 'If you don't like it - lump it.'

Lever, a litigious man at the best of times , sued , and ultimately won an action against the Daily Mirror.

According to some sources Billy Lever was a hopeless soapmaker, and had to bring his own soapboiling specialists to Port Sunlight with him from Warrington . However there is no doubt that William Hesketh Lever was an achiever . Elected to Parliament in 1906, he was made a baronet in 1911, a baron in 1917, and a viscount in 1922. But, like many achievers, their routes to greatness are often obscured. To quote Frederick Schiller the 18th century German writer, " ......history is the world's judgement."

History has many eyes, and the purpose of this book is to look at the 20th century history of this company of 'Billy' Lever's in a different way than has been done before. Through the eyes of those who were there. The ordinary men and women who worked at Billy Levers factory. Those who actually did the work. They made the soap, packed and weighed the products, planned the schedules, recruited the personnel, drove the trucks, lived in the company houses and generally kept the place running.

They too can participate in this historical judgement. It is as valid as any other perspective, if not more so.

An approach was made to the Lever organisation during the creation of this book for the loan of some archive photographs. Such assistance was offered, but only after the company had sight of the text, to ensure that they liked it. In my view, a potential blue pencil upon the text, to veto photograph loans if they didn't approve of the book. The book won the hour. The text is unexpurgated, and manages, I hope, to convey Life at Levers, without the photograph loans from the company.

It seems to me from the outside looking in, that there is a good deal of discontent where there once was harmony of a sort between the company and its workers. Even management people have told me ,'off the record', that the industrial relations at Port Sunlight have 'gone from bad to worse'. Leaner and Meaner is a term our industrialists have borrowed from the United States to describe any new business ethos. 'Levers' is certainly leaner than it once was, employing approximately 1,500 people today. Meaner ? The reader is perhaps the best judge.

This company at one time employed many thousands of people. I have tried hard to talk to those who worked there from all the disparate parts of the whole, and hope that they are representative of all the other workers whose voices are not here.

What follows is about the ordinary men and women who worked at Levers in Port Sunlight within living memory to the present , and what their life was like working at 'Billy' Levers soap factory. Perhaps it is their testimony , the people who actually worked for the company, that can provide the most realistic and untainted view of what this organisation at Port Sunlight was all about.This was Life at Levers.

To them, my thanks, for talking to me. I hope I have done you justice.

David Roberts 1995

*1 BBC Documentary
' Now we're at Port Sunlight' with Russell Harty.

The famous Daily Mirror cartoon of 1906.

Poor Woman: Please Mr Soap Trust, isn't this pound an ounce short?

Mr Soap Trust: Well, what are you going to do about it ? You may think yourself lucky I let you live. I'm boss of the situation, and no one else can make soap except me, and I'll put as few ounces in the pound as I like and raise the price to what I like, and if you don't get out I'll call the Police.

Joyce Maddocks
D.O.B 11.2.26

Messenger Girl - Recruitment Officer, Personnel.

Worked in Levers 1942-1984

I didn't go to Levers first of all. I left Wirral Grammar School and got a temporary job in Woolworth's in New Ferry. It was only a Christmas time job and I went to Levers in the January. I started there on the 26th January 1942, a bitterly cold morning, I think it was snowing. I was fifteen. I had arranged to meet a girl who was already working there as a messenger in the Postal Department.

We were living in Church Drive at that time so I arranged to meet her by the Duke of York's cottages. I was introduced to the Supervisor who was a Miss Roberts and there were several other girls in the Department, two or three of whom I knew. The postal system in those days was that the factory was divided up into four routes A, B, C and D and I was taken out with another girl on one route. She took me round and showed me where to deliver the post, collect the post, put it in a bag and we went round the factory and came back to the Postal Department which in those days was at the back of one of the Production Departments, up a rickety old staircase along a warren of corridors. I went out with her about three times and was then left to go out on my own. I didn't really know what to expect. I had preconceived ideas of what the place was like ,which I'd had since childhood I suppose.

Before the war there were organised tours of the factory and coach parties used to come from all over the North I suppose. Quite a lot from Bolton because the first Lord Leverhulme lived in Bolton so Bolton people came. The assembly point was the Gladstone Hall. The coach parties arrived, the people went in and they had a team of guides who were young ladies, very smartly dressed, had white peaked hats, white coats and gloves and they took parties around. The one thing I can remember about the Gladstone Hall in those days was in the middle of the floor was an enormous globe of the world and there were little lights in every part of the world where there was a Unilever company. What we used to do when we were on school holidays, we used to sneak up there and if the guides knew us they would let three or four of us go in with the main party and that was a regular summer holiday thing. So I had an idea of what it was like inside. I thought it would be great to work there. I thought there was nowhere like it and I'd seen the offices, very long, all the desks were very regimented, each desk had its own reading lamp on and I thought that this was absolutely fantastic. At that time I just wanted to go and learn to be a secretary. Anyway about the fourth or fifth day I was there I was turned loose on this route and got hopelessly lost in the middle of the factory. I think I asked about five people the way back to the Postal Department.

From then on it all fell into place, we learned the other routes and the main idea of having all the postal girls was you did the post in the morning one week and in the afternoon you went to shorthand and typing classes which were in the main office. Then the other week you went to the shorthand and typing classes in the morning and did the post in the afternoon. There were quite a large number of girls there. Then as you progressed in the shorthand and typing you were transferred out to other Departments. There was a central typing pool and then there were vacancies in other departments. I think at that time none of the youngsters in the village really thought of going anywhere else.

It wasn't exactly a closed community but to go to Liverpool at night was a real adventure so people stayed more or less within the confines of the village. There was all sorts of entertainment, clubs and societies. So really you didn't think of other places to go to work. All the parents in the village thought that it was fine for their children to go to Levers. My father and mother had worked there and lived in the village. So you were more or less completely company orientated.

The boys, if they went, they were also recruited as messengers but they started in a special department. So you'd get four or five going in the Time Office, Time and Wages and each department, Engineering, various office departments had their own messenger boys, well they were hopeful of getting apprenticeships. If they didn't then a lot of them went to Cammell Lairds and followed the same pattern, served their apprenticeship, went seafaring for a time, some came ashore and came back here.

It was quite easy to get a job then because it was wartime and people were being called up and going into the forces. You filled an application form in and had an interview and were placed on a waiting list but it wasn't for very long. Even though it wartime it didn't really affect me at work, there were black-outs but everybody got used to it. I know that instead of having an extra hour of daylight we had two extra hours of daylight during the summer. That was really because of the farming community getting the stuff in. I can't remember if there was any similar arrangement in the winter.

It was dark going to work and dark coming home in the winter. In the time I was there we didn't have any day time air-raid warnings. Certainly I don't ever remember going into any of the air-raid shelters so if there were any day time warnings it must have been before 1942. There were underground air-raid shelters right down Wood Street and everybody knew exactly which shelter they had to go to. They were where the flowerbeds are now, also we had identity cards. You had to go through a scrutineers box, there was a row of scrutineers boxes by the main gate and you had to show your card every morning. Then a lot of people went home for lunch so you had to show your card again at lunchtime. I was nearly sixteen then. We'd really had the worst of the air-raids before I started work.

When I first started there it was a multi-national labour force because they were doing contracts for war work, they were making undercarriages for aeroplanes. There were quite a lot of West Indians working at Levers, so that had its problems. At that time there was a West Indian Liaison Officer who had an office in Liverpool and every time there was any trouble they would send for him to come over. It was a man called Leary Constantine, a famous cricketer of that time, a lovely man. There was an Engineering Artificer Section, I can't re-member what they did, it was a war contract. Also they had what was called a Ration Pack Department where they did these tins which went out to the Far East with compact sugar and tea, rations really.

After the war in that Department they did a contract for John Players, stripping the tobacco leaves.

12

They were building back production then. During the war it was the basic soaps so they were getting back into the toilet soap ranges. The tobacco leaf stripping was after the war. It was part time women, they used to strip the leaves, they used to ask for strippers. We used to send these people down for medicals and they would come back with a note - these women are fit for stripping! We even had a notice on the gates - Strippers Wanted. Then after the war all the people who'd gone to the war came back in batches. That must have been traumatic for them, coming back into a shift working system.

After the postal dept. I was sent for and told there was a vacancy in the Personnel Department, but in those days it was called the Service Department in Personnel Records, which although we did shorthand and typing, were all hand-written then and it was a kind of file system where we made out cards for everybody who joined the company. It was just a record system really and filing. The first job I did in Personnel Department was, there was a little annexe and there were thousands of cards which as far as I can remember were a record of people's earnings and tax and these all had to be put in alphabetical order and filed in these filing cabinets. I didn't dislike it but I was completely overwhelmed with the amount of cards there were to do. I started by myself for a couple of days and then somebody else came to help.

There were about eight or nine of us juniors on that particular section and it was quite a detailed record because everything, change of address, when people were off sick ,all went on the card. We would get notes and you'd have to fill in all the relevant details on the card. I enjoyed that, it was quite varied work.

Then one summertime, I was sent to the Employment Bureau, which was known to all and sundry as the "BREW" . That was a building next door to the main gate, it's still there. It had direct access on to the street so that people who came in applying for jobs or who were sent by the Labour Exchange could come straight in without going on to the factory premises. Someone was either off sick or had left, or gone on holiday and I was sent up there for a week and I absolutely loved it. It was interesting work.

It was mainly a bit of typing, working out figures, logging requests for labour, giving out application forms and typing starting papers which were in triplicate and taking the people into the Health Centre for medicals.

So people would come and say I'm looking for a job. Have you got any vacancies they would say. We never said yes we have, We just said, have you filled an application form in and if they had, they were all filed and kept for about three years, we would find the form and bring it up to date and then if they'd been interviewed before we'd say there's nothing suitable, or yes, and then they would start the interview procedure, there and then.

People wouldn't just start there and then. They would come and fill a form in and would be interviewed by the Employment Manager and if he thought they were suitable they would then be taken down to whatever Department they were going to.

Then they would be interviewed by the manager of that department and they would be shown around the department. Then they would come back and we would then arrange for them to come in for a medical examination.

If the medical examination was alright and if they were not already employed they could start the following Monday but if they were employed then obviously they had to work their notice. Then they came along on the Monday, signed their starting papers and were taken to the department. Sometimes they would start them straight away, other times they'd say be in here at 7.45 a.m. on Monday morning and they were left to find their own way down to the Department, later on everybody who started had an Induction course in the Training Department.

Then I went back to Personnel Records for a time and a vacancy came up in the Employment Bureau. The manager then was a Mr Challinor and he asked me if I would like to go and work there and I said I would. He spoke to the Personnel Manager and I was officially transferred to the Employment Bureau.

There was Mr Challinor and about three girls and also a female who interviewed the women but she wasn't domiciled in the building. We recruited people for the factory but the clerical recruitment was done up in one of the wings. Later it all became one. That's how I came to be in Recruitment Department.

I stayed there through all sorts of changes. Eventually they amalgamated it with Training. I didn't really gel with training. We ran courses, Systematic Operator Training Courses. People wrote up their job in a simplified manner. Certain people were selected, senior operator or chargehand level and we gave them a two week training course. At the end of those two weeks they'd not only written a job or two or three jobs in this simplified manner, they'd also been taught how to train someone else to do it. They'd taken that person down and done it.

Those courses I enjoyed very much.

One thing I did find was that you'd be shut away in the Training Department doing the course for a week and it wasn't, to me, the real world. The real world was the Production Department, and going in and out of there. When you came out it made you realise that a lot of people who worked in the office never went into the Production Department. They had no cause to - it was a totally different world. Recruiting for Production, they always wanted people yesterday so you were rushing round. I had to pull all the cards out and write to people. Another thing we had - we had three shifts of part time women, 7 to 12, 12 to 5 and 5 to 10, they would come in perhaps for six weeks, sometimes they'd come in for three weeks. This was after the war when they were getting promotions going. The Production Departments would ring up and say we want eight women on each shift to start next Monday which meant you had to contact the women. If you were lucky they would have been within the period which the medical examination covered , which was about seven to eight months, so they didn't have to have a medical. It meant literally that we used to have to use postcards, one of the juniors would type the postcards, send some through the post, but any local ones would be delivered. I used to ride round at night on my bike delivering these cards. We'd send for eight and they'd tell their friends so we ended up with a waiting room full of people.

We had a bright idea then, we used to send about half a dozen and know that every Wednesday afternoon this lot met up in the market and the word would go round and they would come to us. It was very interesting because the women would always came back to us and they formed groups of people, I still see some of them now, they've kept in touch with each other. These promotions would sometimes be during the school holidays when a lot of them couldn't come because they had no-one to look after the children, so it was pretty hectic. I could never understand why they couldn't plan further ahead but I think at that time it was changing from the old pre-war system where the traveller went to shop and say "Can I sell you four boxes of soap?" but it got that the big buyers were coming in, the supermarkets, and they were dictating how much they wanted. That's why we were getting the pressure.

I preferred recruitment to training. I didn't enjoy the training. I think the worst part was in the latter years during the 70's and 80's, when we didn't have vacancies and people were coming for them and school kids were coming from school. I didn't enjoy that at all, because they were the type of people who were unemployed who a few years ago would have been snapped up. What Levers did was they started a non-recruitment policy. They reduced the numbers by natural wastage so there were no mass redundancies because they just let the numbers run down. That was a sad part. I loved the job all the time I did it, but the best years, the best times, were after the war and the 60's because they were building the Company up again. The whole atmosphere of the place was great. When early retirement first came in a lot of people didn't want to go simply because they'd never thought of it. In the early years it was no hassle to go to work on a Monday morning, you couldn't get in quick enough. I don't think I was the only one because people say now that they loved it, it was great.

Now it's changed completely. I don't think anybody feels their job's that secure. The best boss I ever had was a woman, Dorothy Bridgewood, and she was the female Recruitment Officer and I was working in the Department then as a shorthand typist and clerk. I started doing preliminary interviews so when they came I would check the cards and pass them into her. Then gradually I took on part of her job when she went off sick or on holiday. She was a fantastic person to work for, one of the few women in high positions apart from the Health Centre and Catering. I don't think there were many women bosses then. The boss I was most afraid of was probably because it was all so different then, but I think probably the woman who was in charge of the Postal Department. I was absolutely terrified of her. Her name was Miss Roberts. She ruled with a rod of iron.

There were still plenty of laughs though. I can remember one story. In Records, where I'd worked originally, it was always manned by young girls and they had a Supervisor there who was very fussy, very efficient. We were talking in the office one day about if you told a person that they didn't look very well eventually that person would begin to feel ill, convince themselves they're not feeling very well. So we said it's like if you say you can smell something. They decided to get this Supervisor going. In the corridor outside there was a wooden block floor and underneath was the central heating pipes. There were metal strips which the men used to lift to get at these pipes if there was anything wrong and of course the rats used to get down there and would suffocate. So these kids went back and said "Oh, there's a funny smell down here". The Supervisor was going round saying he couldn't smell anything. "Oh yes". He said , "I've told you girls about leaving sandwiches half eaten in the drawer, somebody's sandwiches have gone off. I'm sick of telling you about it". So one of them rang me and told me to go down there, casually, so I went strolling in and he's on top of the filing cabinet with a stick poking at something at the back. I asked what he was doing and they said "Well he thinks there's something down there that's smelling". The next thing he says "I know what it is - I can smell it, it's a dead rat. Get Ratty Price".

In the meantime he goes down to the Toilet Soap Department where they used to wrap the luxury soaps in an absorbent paper and it was heavily perfumed. He got a sheet of this paper, cut it into strips and gave all the girls a piece of this paper. We had all the ducting up but never found a dead rat. One of the girls stuck a piece of this paper under the collar of his coat. He came in the next morning and said "You know that paper is very heavily perfumed, I could smell it all night at home". There was always something going on, practical jokes. The messenger boys were the worst. Of course they had the usual things, they'd be sent down to blow in this machine and came back with two black eyes, the other thing was the long stand. I was surprised they ever fell for that but they did.

I remember the first strike they had, the Building Department. We weren't involved in any negotiations or anything like that and they were standing outside the main gate when we were going into work. They were very aggrieved because the gateman wouldn't let them go in to get a cup of tea from the vending machine. They'd just chosen to walk out. That would be about late 70's I think. It was all over in a day I think. I thought it was a bit daft. The company were very good, the Company's attitude changed but I don't think it was the company so much as management that changed. When the experienced managers retired or left they were replaced by younger managers, the whole face of Industrial Relations changed.

My last two years there saw a lot of changes in management, recruitment was nonexistent and I was happy to retire. When the first offer of early retirement came out I decided to take it. I never regretted it but I never regretted any of the time I spent there. But today's climate is very different, I wouldn't work there again now. They're not the caring Company they used to be. When I started the Company was very paternal both inside the factory and as a tenant living in the village. They were there for you It wasn't that you thought the Company would provide but it was a paternalistic attitude. When I was there, there were people of two or three generations so they had the same attitude to the Company as I did. I doubt now there's anybody left.

People coming in are coming from an entirely different world, graduates. The whole attitude is different. It's got to change, it couldn't stay as it was .The whole idea of the beautiful village , and providing houses if you work there was, for that time, alright. I've heard both sides of the argument. There were certain rules and regulations and if kids misbehaved the fathers were hauled up in front of management but when you see the way some of them vandalise now it's not such a bad thing, although it would never work now.

When my time's up the company will sell my home off. I had an option to buy it once but decided not to. Looking back I thought at one time I was a fool not to but my father was alive then and he'd been ill for many years and to me having always lived in rented accommodation and at that time mortgages being an entirely different world, I was coming up to retirement and I didn't think I would be able to pay back a mortgage. A house was offered to sitting tenants for £12,000 in the late 70's, early 80's and that was quite a lot of money. Afterwards I thought maybe I should have bought it but there's also the expense of upkeep. All these houses are listed buildings and if you go round and look at some of the chimneys, if they have to be replaced they have to be replaced in exactly the same way which is very expensive, it all depended on the state of the house.

Even now, it's the little things like when you're 80 years old you get a birthday card and a bouquet or something, I mean why wait until you're 80? A lot of people now feel that once you're gone you're gone and that's it. It never used to be like that. There were things for the pensioners and they were respected. I feel that pensioners on the whole are forgotten. I've been away from it for 12 years now but quite frankly I couldn't stand the pace. There were attitudes that I'd never been used to. Integrity went, in many, many ways and I couldn't be doing with that. You could trust people, you knew they wouldn't let you down but with some of the latter people you just didn't know, you looked out for yourself. That was the great thing, you worked for management that you respected. That type of management changed. Attitudes changed.

Irene Mounsey
D.O.B 5.1.24

Process Operator
Checkweigher

Worked in Levers
1963-1984

I remember on my first day it was frightening, going down the steps into number one soap room, getting out an overall, one of the kind that you tie at the back, putting on a turban because you had to wear turbans then like scarves, you tied up. I remember going into see the machines and when I started they were first making "Dual", it was when everyone used to have linos years ago, going back about 34 years, it use to put a shine on all your linos, it was a liquid and if you put it on it gave your lino a shine, weren't all carpeted then like this, most people had a carpet and a lino round the edges. First of all I think we were doing some samples, that was the start, they don't make it now as nobody has linos do they? That was our first job.

I remember, I was wrapping up some of the Lux, I think it was giving them a holiday, going cheap, or had a special offer on the wrappers. They used to give you papers to wrap around the things. I wasn't on the Dual machines, I was on the wrapping as there were some other girls already there on the Dual . I wasn't exactly frightened, but when you haven't worked in a factory before, or haven't worked for a long time, it was my first job since I had been married, but we were all in the same boat. You couldn't wear jewellery, some used to say.... why can't I , but it was understandable really why. There were quite a few girls working at Levers at the time and I was thinking, ... well I tell you why I had moved there, I had , and I think Bill had been out on strike and I was thinking, Oh God we have got all the rates to pay and that and I thought I could get a little job. So I went up with one of the girls that lived on the estate , she got started because her husband worked there, and we had our names down so we also got sent for.

My friend Doreen Sindall started with me, and we've been friends ever since. All the girls were great there . I believe it is not the same now, when I meet anybody that's there now , they say we don't have the laughs that we used to . We worked hard, but I really liked it . I enjoyed it, but they don't have the same laughs now. It fitted in with the children, I didn't have to rely on other people. I had to get the bus and couldn't be late , or say one wasn't too good it could be a problem. But I could give them all their tea, wash up and see them all home from school safe, and Bill would be home then. That means a lot and I could go to work with a clear conscience.

It was a five o'clock start. There were always plenty of buses when we came out at finishing time at 10 o'clock. Because we were in number 1 we were nearer the bus, so we were able to run out to dash onto the first bus , if you were in another part of the factory you'd have to get the next one along but they were always reliable. They'd be there waiting when we came out. When we arrived at 5 o'clock there would be a great big long line of buses there waiting to take the day workers home. There used to be eight or nine thousand people in the factory in those days. We didn't all have cars then. I was home for about 10.15 p.m. and then Bill got a car and he'd pick me up and I was home for five past ten.

It was a great firm to work for ! We all had young children , and we were all coming out to work to earn a bit more and give our children a little bit , go on holidays. When you buy a new house after coming from a small house there's a lot to be done isn't there. I didn't meet anybody horrible there at all , they were all my friends. We had a quarter of an hour tea break, and we used to do all sorts in that quarter of an hour tea break. After Christmas time , when things were dull ,we would have a tramps ball, it sound silly , but in that quarter of an hour ,we all took our things in , get dressed up in our stuff and walk in while all the girls were having their tea and we gave all the girls a laugh. At Easter we would do an Easter bonnet parade, not all of the girls, only the ones that were game for a laugh sort of , just in that quarter of an hour, but you'd be surprised what you can do in that short time . We always put fancy hats on. We had a little party for the Jubilee too. I was a bit of a Royalist and they started to call me the Queen Mother , because we used to see pictures of Charles and I'd always say ah! Isn't he lovely.

I always used to have the aspirins for the girls too, if they ever had a headache or anything. Sometime the fellas too would say go and ask Irene , she'll have an aspirin. When we first started there was only a couple of machines. Then we came onto the big machines, and you worked on the lines then. As a checkweigher I worked on two machines. As the things came down I had to take off how ever many heads the machine had on and check the weights for any light weights . If there were lights , you had to stop that pallet to be checked, or if labels weren't right or labels were missing it was the same procedure. Of course it's all automatic machines these days. They don't have checkweighers now, they have things to automatically throw the light weights off.

We had a mixed tea room, but the men didn't have their tea with us. At the beginning it was only a ladies room. When we first started there they used to have a lady who would give you tea , a free cup of tea.

I liked the job I was doing, checkweighing, because being on two machines I was walking around have my little chats, whilst also doing the work. On another night I might change to two different machines . Different weeks I was on different machines. It was good.

If you had a bad job you'd always be working with another person so you could have a laugh and so they would take away the badness of the job. We didn't like going in when we had to clean and wash off the labels. We had these big tanks. A pallet might have been stopped because the labels were wrong somehow , we had to put them into big tanks of hot water and scrub all the labels off . They could be Stergene or Handy Andy in plastic bottles, that sort of thing. We weren't too keen on that job. But it was a job. Anything that had a label on it, the labels also had to be straight. It didn't happen that often, it used to be some girls only job , but if a machine had finished they'd say , right all into the waste area , it was called the waste area.

We had men over us. Sam Hazelhurst , then we had Mr. West , then we had Alan Millington. I liked Alan Millington, he was younger than me, and went Rock Ferry High School and I knew another boy that went to school with him. He was all right. I had another boss, Ted Sumner and poor old Ted passed away. Ted used to be in the army and he used to give a shine to his shoes. He was always joking with the girls and asking them to stand over his shoes so he could check the shine.

The chargehand was Jessie Parker. She was very strict. You knew were you stood with her, if you did anything wrong she would tell you so. She'd say " and you Irene, you should know better, because you've been here longer." She'd say that to you even if you hadn't done anything wrong. She was dead strict but she was fair. I didn't mind that. We were a little scared of her. But when we always went on nights out with the girls to a pantomime or something she'd always come out with the girls and she was a different person. But at work she was the boss. She wouldn't let you be picked upon by somebody else, she never had her favourites, which is a good thing. I was a bit frightened of her.

We girls used to go out on Saturdays. I was the one who used to organise them. We went to see a pantomime , The Empire or the Royal Court, we'd go out for a dinner at the Lord Nelson , We always used to get the front row and all sat in the front seats, all fifty of us, well you can imagine. We used to have a fine time, we saw Ken Dodd and all sorts of people. Then we'd have a drink at The Lord Nelson, but we would always get the last train home over the river. We all used to sing on the last train home.

I really liked the company and the girls. I was lucky as a checkweigher , some of the girls would have to put the caps on the bottles, all night, that must have been a boring job. You had to have your laughs and do things because factories are boring places really. The chaps were very good. There were a lot more of them towards nearer the end, but you know, I never really heard any bad language spoken. Even if they were talking to another man and they swore , they'd apologise to you. They always used to say sorry even if they weren't talking to me. They were all very generous people too. The money when we first started wasn't much, it wasn't even five pound when we started, but in 1963 , when I used to work 25 hours, 5 nights a week it was a bit of money. I was lucky and kept well because if a woman's going to work and she's not well then that's hard.

I worked in number one where the liquids were. I believe it was the first room in the factory that was built. You used to have to go down the steps into it , and it was very warm down there. There was no air once and they couldn't get the blowers working then, so they used to give us barley water to drink, it was that hot you were unable to work. Tony Maclean , the union man, came in and said that he thought we should all go home. So we all took his advice and went ; that was the only time I walked out. I think we did get paid in the end for it. I think the union sorted that out. We never had strikes. I once took an hour off like everyone else did for the nurses, Tony Maclean said to just take an hour off.

I'd do it again .Yes. Being honest it suited me with the children. It was a factory so when I came out I had no worries did I. When you're a factory worker, a process worker , you go to work , you do your work and you come home. I had four children. If you worked somewhere else with other responsibilities then you are thinking of those responsibilities away from your work aren't you. I didn't want other responsibilities I didn't want to take more on. I had the children. I maybe could take responsibilities now , but I'm too old now. And they don't have checkweighers anymore.

I feel as though I could work now. It wouldn't be the same though now, they don't have checkweighers. I don't work there now but I believe it's not the same anymore. I was at a retirement party last week, Margaret Glover and her husbands retirement. There were lots of girls there and I was sitting next to one chap who was still there and he was saying it was not the same now Irene you wouldn't know it , you wouldn't like it. What he means I don't know.

Everybody there now seems to be there just for the money. Of course we all go to work for the money, but we had something else. It's only the money that is keeping them there really. Now I believe they have to clock on and off every different job they do, they have to wear little name tags and be accounted for everywhere you go. We never did that. A boss would just say .... go over to number four on a message or whatever, and you'd just go and do it. Although we worked hard and before we went home we had to wash around our machines on our hands and knees. In the early days, we used to clean, really we did, a girl would cover you whilst you did your job. The machines were still going but they weren't fast machines. We called them piston machines. The polys used to come along and you'd take two, hold them up to be filled. Then down. Then the next two and so on. They have machines now that will do in an hour or so what would take us all week or two weeks to do. That's automation.

When I was there we still had the piston machines. There were about 10 or 11 girls on a line. There was another room that had the faster machines, they had about five girls on them. I believe there are now only three people who work on all of the really fast machines. We did all the liquids, Comfort, Sunlight, Stergene, Handy Andy. The girls on the Bexuda machine did the bigger drums of liquid for factories , hospitals and that. That was heavier work and they had to do a lot of lifting , but they all liked the jobs that they were doing. They were all in their own little groups you see.

I remember things like Jesse telling us off for smoking in the toilets. She'd shout .... Hey ! No smoking in here you lot.

I have no regrets about working there, they were all nice people, met nice friends, such good times we had. In the early days they'd go around with a van with a loudspeaker on the top of it asking if anyone wanted a job.

When I was leaving I knew I'd miss all my friends but I accepted it, I used to go back for all the other retirements. I did enjoy going there when I went to work. I used to talk about going back. I see Val at the club occasionally , and the other girls, Doreen , Delsie and Joan , my friends , we all go out a couple of times each year. We phone each other. We all used to sit at the table , the same friends.

We were in number one, but it all altered even before I went, automation, they are all like robots. But it has got to change I suppose.

I enjoyed it. You had your moans, and sometimes , oh poor Jessie, she might be in a mood, but you knew where you stood and that was it. We had many great times. You always knew were you stood. You can't go to work and it would always be perfect. Sometimes it would all run smoothly, then sometimes everything would be light and it would all go wrong.

Well I don't know, when you see and hear about it, it does not seem the same. It's not a happy place I believe. You go past the factory now it and it all seems dead.

A group Photo outside 'the room' Irene Mounsey is kneeling third from the left.

The girls at work, stopped here for a presentation. Irene is standing in the first row, 5th from left. Jessie Parker is standing on the far right.

Eric Coates

D.O.B 26.5.43

Mechanical Fitter

Worked in Levers
1959-Present

I had to take a second interview to be an apprentice fitter because first off I was in the printing trade. You actually apply to the Trades Unions, the Chapels, and I wanted to be a printer basically, and Levers, well they used to take apprentices on a twice a year intake, and they used to take them right across the whole range of skills. In the printing there were printer apprentices, compositor apprentices, book-binding apprentices, electro stereo-type apprentices . . . the compositor used to make the print, at least they did in 1958, the compositor used to set the print up and then they used to use like a straw set up when I arrived there. That would give you the imprint of the plate. That used to be sprayed and put in an oven and the plastic would mould itself to the print, then they would spray it with silver or nickel and put it in a copper sulphate bath. Then they'd peel this thin strip of copper off and they would plate it and fill the back with electro metal and that would then become a flatbed printing plate. The flatbed machines were used in the production of the Persil packets of the day.

I applied through the Trades Unions for the electro stereo-type job in conjunction with Levers and started the six-year apprenticeship in 1958. The Union dues were £1 a week. Lever's took the shortfall. The printing trades, they only had five Chapels, the Liverpool Chapel, Cardiff, London, Glasgow and Manchester Chapels. Each part of the Chapel used to send how many people they needed. Say the whole country needed 20 apprentices, they used to start 15, so there was always a demand. They were duty bound in the printing trade then that if you applied for a job, and you didn't think it was enough money, you told your Chapel, which in this case was Liverpool, and like the Branch Committee of the AEU, they sat in their wisdom and if they supported you, that job was blacked and you virtually went back on your own money.

Lever's applied to the electro stereo-type union and said we require an apprentice and that was how it was done. Lever's have always been trades-unionised, it's an amazing company for that. There's never been any problem with Trades Union membership. Billy Lever himself was unionised early on. The Unions never had to bang on the door , with old Billy Lever. I've still got a copy of the agreement he made. There was nothing to see on the notice board and they didn't advertise through the local press so much then. Painters, plumbers, fitters, electricians, boiler makers, sheet metal workers, wheelwrights, all the printing trades, iron workers. That's how I started and then I transferred to engineering.

Vauxhalls wasn't open. I went to Lairds for an interview, we all did. I went to New Chester Road School and it seemed like . . . no disrespect to anybody, it would be great if those days came back . . . the thing for a secondary modern school lad who was reasonable was an apprenticeship and like a lot of us I applied to Cammell Laird, Van den Burghs and Lever Brothers. My dad worked at Lever Bros. I got in as an electro stereo-type apprentice . He thought it was a good idea for me, because he wasn't a tradesman. I don't think he was that bothered where I worked, it was just a job. They were good apprenticeships to have. As far as I can remember I just walked into the place , you'll think I'm making it up but I'm certainly not, going back to the electro stereo-typing, it was 8 till 4 in 1958, so I walked in behind everybody else. People used to run down the road past me and clock me on because they used to think I was a dope. Today everybody starts at 10 to 8 till half five. The electro stereo-typing agreement with Levers was 8 till 4. They did themselves out of work in the end. Fellow called Anelly was the first boss. I don't know where he is now. Did the usual, follow Nelly, you know. There was an apprentice just out of his apprenticeship. He'd just come back from the marines and there was a fifth year lad.

The first job they put me on was working with a guy called Norman Maudsley, Tommy Weaver, Kevin Cross was the lad who'd just finished his National Service, he was the headbanger of the gang, George Brown, his brother still works in research. He was the FOC, Father of the Chapel. The first job was just watching George back printing plates basically with the electro metal. So that was my first day, six months or so we did that for. It was a good idea at the time, a good apprenticeship.

It was only in later years I became a shop steward. Especially on the printing side it was a very well paid job and it was just a job. There was no day release for the printing trades, I had to go to night - school Mondays and Fridays. I even left early for night school. No it couldn't have been 8 till 4 it must have been 8 till 5. That's right it was 8 till 5 and the factory was 7.50 to 5.30. The foundry was 8 till 5 and because the night-school was the Liverpool College of Art ,there wasn't a printing college this side of the water, I used to go at 4 o'clock on nights - school night. I would say, relatively speaking as an apprentice, I thought I was in clover then because they did look after apprentices.

Pretty soon after I saw another side to life there , because after six months my indentures were required to be backdated, I've still got the letters from the District Committee of the AEU, all the correspondence between Bert Rule and Lever Bros.

There were thousands working there then and there seemed to be fewer tradespeople. A guy came to see me last Saturday who was the first fitter I ever worked with. I took him down to Chelsea Flower Show for his 70th birthday, he's 78 now, fellow called Lennie Rowlands, he was the first fitter I ever worked with. The first job I was on with Lennie was Lux Flakes. Comparing it to the print trades there was a big difference , anybody can teach engineering or fitting, if they knew what they were doing . Technically, you don't even have to have served an apprenticeship, but in the printing trade you had to be a member of a Print Shop, so printing apprentices didn't go to the training centre at Port Sunlight. Fitter apprentices did, so I did six months in the printing factory and the foundry and when I was transferred I then went to the training centre at Port Sunlight. Then when I left the training centre the first place I actually worked was the machine shop. I was working on lathes and shaping machines with a fellow called Bob Mason who showed me the ropes.

The worst job I've had there is probably the one I've got now. Now it's going down the pan. I'm 52 now so I've got to get at least three more years in. With the Unilever Pension Fund if you go between 50 and 55 for every year you go early you lose 5%. So I would lose 15% now, you see. It's hard to think about doing a job where the boss would say.... that's a really good job that , well done Eric ......Working shift work it's never worked that way, has it? Because you go in and whatever the job is you do it during the duration of your shift, if you haven't finished then your mate takes over. I've been on shift work since I was 21, so really there's never been a dedicated job. There's three of you on three shifts and on four shifts there's four of you .

I've worked that way certainly all my married life and I was on it before I was married, and I've been married 26 years. All in all I liked shift work, it was very enjoyable. Good for hobbies, good when the children were young too, I'd take them to school, meet them from school, that was good. The problem with night shifts is lack of sleep and all that, but I managed to get through it. Haven't got a problem with shift work , I don't look bad on it do I ? The ability to sleep anywhere anytime is a great plus, I spent a lot of time with my family.

I'm not really a boss person because Lever Bros. is the iron hand in the velvet glove. In my time I've seen bosses come and then they go. I'm of the belief that all bosses are there to do you down and if you can get a reasonable deal off them then you've won one, you know. Not just now either, the old school Lever bosses were difficult, as are the new ones, but there were bosses everywhere and they could make or break you. If I had to choose between the old style bosses and the new style then I'd take the older one because for all their iron hand they were a little bit fairer. I would say they were a little bit fairer. There was the common decency of the working life then, where people with youngsters were seen as needing money more than somebody say whose children had left home. That decency has gone down the pan. That's nothing unique to Lever Bros., that's unique to life isn't it, the way the lads and ladies looked out for each other has gone. Everybody just fights their own corner now.

The present bosses are different. I would say the present management is the worst. Because of their inability to manage the way the job is. We only work four days, we work a banked hour system now, Monday to Thursday and we bank the Friday to cover for 12 hours you see , so when you are on a 3 shift situation if your mate's off, through sickness, holidays, whatever, then you work 12 hours you see. You don't get paid, there's no overtime anymore. It's an annualised hour situation. The job is that slack. I'm talking about bosses from the top to the bottom. We only work Monday to Thursday.

I'm a shop steward. Things developed that way because of the way we were being treated at a particular time when Lever Bros. wanted to reintroduce enzymatic production, that's enzymes. They had a terrible press in the 1960s where there were people injured making some of the detergents . Our competitors, Proctors, held their hands up and said well we'll both come out of that side of the business ...... which they did do. Levers had enzymes on the shelf and then they wanted to reintroduce them in such a terrible manner. Basically the shop steward in the area I was working wasn't up to it and he resigned , and actually left us with a bit of a problem on our hands.

So , I grasped the nettle and went as a shop steward from there on until the present day which must be fifteen years, more or less. The company didn't seem to be dealing with us in what I would say was a responsible manner at that time. They were trying to kid us. The same process is still in use today. Now people still have to have a medical every 12 months because under the Health & Safety At Work Act, it does have capabilities of forming industrial asthma . I would say in part because of the stance of myself and others, we did get a set of procedures which we still abide by today. There has been conflict too . I've been out of the gate twice. The AEU and the electricians, yes. We're amalgamated these days, we're now the AEEU. It is a company that hasn't had much industrial unrest but certainly the engineering unions have given them a run for their money. We're proud of it in a way, the engineering have given then a run for their money. Levers weren't used to it. It was settled in a couple of days. We've had work to rules and we've actually been in dispute, probably a week at the most.

We weren't afraid to do it, and the management didn't take too kindly to it , no they didn't. The last time we went out the gate was the centenary year 1988 , believe it or not. I don't know whether you've been in the factory, in the vestibule it's like a stately home, with the two figureheads, Darcy Lever one side and Billy Lever the other side and we were actually having our meeting at 8 o'clock and we were threatening to do a walk and the band was playing , the Port Sunlight Brass Band in the vestibule playing Abide with me, and I used the analogy that it was like the iceberg sailing towards the Titanic, the band playing. We were actually in dispute when I was with Russell Harty on his show that he did about Lever's. We had the officials in at the time. . . because of the way they were treating us.

There've been cock-ups and accidents occasionally, I've had a few myself. Had a very bad one with an chemical substance in both eyes. I attended St Paul's for a number of days and fortunately got through it but I lost my vision for two or three days. It was through opening a vessel up that hadn't been completely drained or something. We've had people burnt, scalded. It's the same in every process. We certainly haven't had the likes of accidents that maybe Cammell Laird have with people falling off things.

They still have a health centre. In fact they've just moved the nursing cover down from four shift to three shift. They still have a dentist and a doctor. They've just finished with the X-ray recently. They have a dentist, chiropody, a well-man clinic too. I've got to go for mine next week, where they show you a video at the end of it "Get to know your scrotum". As you know, it's a poor fitter who doesn't examine his scrotum at least six times a shift.

Me and an old friend of mine , Jeff Rickards, did some research once, over the Storeton Tramway , 'cause that's what Jeff was interested in , and Jeff had an introduction into an a very old-established family in Port Sunlight, although I'm not sure what generation it would be, but this old dear was in her seventies, I'm sure. Whether or not it was her grand or great-grandfather, but they told a story of when the war was on. The Bromborough Pool was primarily used for loading stone from the quarry, the great-grandfather was responsible for loading the stone barges, so he had like the checker's office, for want of a better word, on the quay, and they told the story of Billy Lever knocking on the door with his silver handled cane and wanted them out, off the premises, because he started to buy up the land, he just mobbed the area, didn't he?

He offered them the tenancy of the first house built to get them out of the way. The same lady then went onto the business. Before they built the offices, when his office was in No. 1, he used to do the book-keeping every Friday. They used to do the book-keeping on a Friday and I think he had five accountants and himself . The shape of his office was such , that no-way did the others know what money was going through the business as he had the master book and his accounting was unique, that's how he skimmed the money off the top, because as you probably know he went bust a couple of times and Darcy the other brother bailed him out. He sailed a bit close to the wind did old Billy Lever.

Some say he was paternalistic, and there were a lot of great people in that era. He was certainly a visionary. He had it sewn up. He certainly got his pound of flesh didn't he? There was another story about the boots and the window, where if you were sick, to show you weren't swinging the lead you had to show your boots in the window.

When they first started building the village it was a lot smaller than it is now and he knew every employee and knew where they lived, and if you were sick, legend has it that he would pass the house in his coach and horses, because that's the way he came to work from the manor, came down the Causeway, he came to the stable yard, that's where the shop is now, Gladstone Hall, and he would go out of his way to look at all the houses in the village and to show the people weren't playing hooky they used to put their boots in the window, because the working man only had one pair of boots. So they couldn't be doing anything else that they shouldn't have been. That was the story.

It was a similar tale with the church and the pub. Did they want a church or did they want a pub? The residents said they wanted a pub so he made it a six day house. The Bridge Inn was a six day house and you must remember when it was closed on Sundays when he owned it because some of the workers used to clock on in there.

Billy Lever seems to have been a great "hedger of bets", nobody screwed him , or was able to screw him because he had the rail network into the factory, his own railway, his own transport and barges.

I've no real regrets about working there for 30 odd years now, no, not really. It's been a reasonable job. A reasonable life , yes. I'm more or less happy but not at the present. I'm certainly not happy with the present - since they've launched the dreaded Horizon 2000, we all call it Horror-Zone 2000 , it's been a mess to what it was. Horizon 2000 is a state of play, if you like, the abolition of working life as we knew it and we went into this new agreement with no demarcation - abolition of proper money-earning opportunities, namely overtime. We work annualised hours. Generally it's just a free for all now , which ain't working. The company's broken every rule in the book. We tend to have honoured every rule in the book but at the moment things are I would say . . . we're getting a little bit jumpy, especially the way the business is going, with this Persil Power problem and what it does , allegedly , to the washing. That's been dragged through the media. It's not for sale any more, they changed it to New Generation.

The new working practices are certainly not to my liking, through Horror-Zone 2000. I'm very proud of the trade and the thought of somebody else doing it isn't on. I'm not a Luddite because I was one of Lever's first thinkers in multi-skills. We had a multi-skills before that, with electricians training as fitters etc. Any agreement that says there will be no artificial demarcation gives you problems, doesn't it?

It's hard to work out if you'd do it all again isn't it, because life's moved on a step hasn't it? I would say not, wouldn't I, because I had that first experience as an electro stereo-typer and fitter. I would certainly like to be a fitter again, I had no regrets in that whatsoever. I've enjoyed being a fitter and I still do, I still work with my hands. I would be a fitter again anytime. I Never applied for a job, or a promotion at all. Basically still a Rag-arse. With a capital R if it goes in the book.

I wouldn't get a job there now. They took the multi-skill apprentices on the agreement that they were looking out for A level people. We worked with apprentices who've got HND in electrical and mechanical engineering. But even if that wasn't the case , and I'd just left school again today , under the present agreement, I wouldn't want to know, because of the things I've mentioned .They've changed the new working practices in the last three years so I wouldn't.

If I had that potential, I'd go to university. If you had enough A levels, the ability, not only to serve a hands-on apprenticeship but to spend two and a half years at Chester College as well and get your HND in electrical and mechanical engineering, you're wasted in a factory on a shop floor. It's still factory life. They develop people to this unbelievable level but when they shout you still jump. Youngsters rebel - there's only one left from the first intake. They all went. One went to computers and another went to university.

I stayed and am still there because the money was consistent. Nothing else but. I was married at 24 years old and the money was there every week wasn't it. When Vauxhalls started up there was an exodus from the likes of Lever Bros. to Vauxhalls and to building Polaris submarines at Lairds . There was better money there. The money at Levers just rolled in. It's not loyalty it's basic facts of life. It wasn't easy , doing 30 years on shift. I have been outside though , got a balanced view of things I hope , I worked at Foxhalls in Norfolk Street, they're still in business in the Queens Dock area I think , doing ships winches and derricks , I went to sea for a few trips .

But I stayed at Levers for all this time because the money just keeps rolling in. I still enjoy being a fitter. I haven't got fed up with my lack of promotional opportunities. I'm still doing the same job as I did when I was serving my time, although engineering's changed, but I would just say that the money was there and a lad like me just carried on.

I never got a Lever house in the village because I never really liked them. I don't know if the opportunity was ever there, really. It never entered my head. My parents lived in the Village but it never entered my head to live there. Anything me mum and dad said I went to the opposite anyway. Not a lot wrong with that is there? I wasn't interested because I didn't like the houses. Nicer on the outside than on the inside, they are very poky. When Russell Harty made a T.V. programme about the village , I think I said to him somewhere along the line, that Lord Leverhulme would turn over in his grave if he knew what they were doing with the houses. As a village , it was a captive labour force for Billy Lever wasn't it? We have had it at union meetings, You can see it there , you can see the people who stood to lose their house, they weren't going to put their hand up to do a walk.

I'm as certain as you can be that I'll see out my working days there. At 52 I'm the third oldest in the gang at our shop so it just shows ... at Prices if you were 50 you were an old man. At Lever Bros. for the first time ever they have made people compulsorily redundant. They have a fifteen years' service award where you get a clock or a canteen of cutlery or a set of glasses, and 25 years you used to get a month's average pay, because all pay is average now. They used to do secondments , preparing for retirement , to Ness Gardens, Wirral Borough Council and the Boat Museum but they don't do that any more.

I could sever from the place quite easily though. The redundancies are done on a point system where there were so many points on an objective basis and so many on subjective, the objective being disciplinaries, punctuality - I've always been red-hot on time-keeping. Providing you got into work on time you had a job there for life. The subjectives were team-working, technical ability and the third one escapes me and a number of people fell in the catchment area and below that level they said they were the people at risk of being made redundant and people above it were safe. The likes of myself had to go in and appeal for these people's jobs and there's nothing more soul-destroying, especially to appeal for a person you've worked alongside for 20 years and lose it. It takes part of you , that basic human decency. The soul the shop stewards must have for their fellow people - to lose cases like that does have an impact on you and it conditions your mind as well for future events.

I could part company with my chums, no messing, that won't bother me at all, when the time comes. I'm still a bit of a loner, I won't have my meal break with anybody, I sit on my own. I'm not cliquey. I'm very much my own person. When the day comes and the next Saturday is not a shift pattern day and that's it , I'm going to be absolutely delighted. I'm going to sell up and move out. Yes. Going to go somewhere nearer the Equator. The Wirral's a nice area to grow but I'd like to be somewhere where you can grow a few more tender plants, I like my plants you know. As they say in the trade, a plant fitter.

Some would say I was slightly unhinged anyway, although I can live with that.

Eric and 'the lads' messing about in the Electrical workshop in 1976. The hats are made from rolls of corrugated card. Eric is seated on the far right.

Frank Birks
D.O.B 6.6.45

H.G.V Driver

Worked in Levers
1977-1989

I was 32 when I came to Levers from Cadburys. I did eight months at Cadburys as a delivery driver and the day I started at Cadburys they decided to move to St Helens . Lever Bros. contacted Cadburys to see if they had any drivers available as they were starting their own van fleet up. That's how I came to get an interview, because Levers was , really and truly , a hell of a job to get into as a driver you know. Good firm.. I'd always worked for the likes of Crutchleys , which was low paid , hard hours and you daren't open your mouth or you were sacked .There you could be begging for just a rope, and they say ..... but we gave you a rope three years ago , where's that ?.....

A guy called Gordon Sutcliffe was the boss at Levers then , he interviewed me and gave me the job. They took about four drivers from Cadburys. They were just starting their delivery fleet of vans , which were multiple deliveries , from Leeds to Stoke, but in a concentrated area. They were new vehicles , and it was something new to me to have a new vehicle. It was new to me to get a new overall. Levers did everything right setting up a new fleet. The maintenance on the vehicles was good too, and the pay was very good

It was an entirely different atmosphere, I was used to delivering for small companies for low wages and bad conditions. The first day you started at Levers, you were taken into the office, then you had a medical, were measured for overalls and that. You got two sets of overalls, gloves and things like that which I wasn't used to at all.

They say that the grass in greener on the other side , and I used to

attend   union meetings as a young driver, and listen to the Levers lads
talking about their wages. They would always opt out of the vote if it
was for more money or anything like that , because it didn't matter to
them, they were on such good money anyway. We all used to look at
them lads and think 'stuffy bastards '... and then it happened to me. I
remember coming home and showing my wife Lynne my uniform , saying
they'd given us two uniforms , they'd put us out with drivers to show us
the job for a month ,

They might not admit it , but Levers scheduled all their wagons
for a 12 hour day, and there was no overtime unless you broke down.
The load planners would say they were planning you an eight hour
day, but everyone of us always did 11 or 12 hours. I talk to my own lad
now, when he moans about doing 12 hours in his office , and I did that
for years and years at Levers.

You never came back in before 12 hour either , if you finished in
say 10 hrs , you didn't come back in . I wasn't in the union then , although
later I became a senior steward. If you came back in early the union
would say to you .. what are you doing coming back in ?... I took a
while to get into the system of doing things like that, it wasn't like
Crutchleys expected all the time, when you were rushing around to get
things done.

It was so easy going in Levers it was unbelievable. We had a
boss called Norman Evans, been there 40 years and didn't have much
time to go, so we never got any trouble off him. To the likes of me and
lads that had come from outside, like Cadbury's , it was a dream job. It
would be wrong of me to say I always wanted to go to work. I didn't
want to go to work when the rain was hitting the windows. But once I
was in Levers , I loved the job. I loved multi deliveries. In later life I
ended up on the artics , that didn't appeal too much , just going from A
to B or to Warrington three times a day.

The company was brilliant. In many ways it was too soft really,
I can say that. You'd walk in offices and see a little guy sitting there at
a desk , and if you asked folks what he did , most people didn't know
what he did, and he was there day after day after day . It was a standing
joke there over the lads with the green cards for the toilet would be on
12 hours. It was a sort of medical certificate , like a disabled person.
The company had to employ a certain number of disabled people.
They were getting x pound a week and were "toilet technicians."

When I started as a vanman, there were guys who had come
back after the war , who had never had to pass a H.G.V. Licence, they

just had what they used to call the heavy haulage. They worked the artics which was the soft touch , all they did was to go to the docks and sit there all day until they unloaded you , or just wind your curtains back or take the ropes off. When the van fleet arrived , some of them , but not all of them, about three quarters of them treated us like second class citizens. Then once we'd felt out feet , we were a bigger voice than they were at union meetings because there were more of us. Even then , they'd time taking any sick time off to make sure no van drivers could get onto their artics. They resented vans drivers going onto artics. We could do it , most of us were class 1, but they didn't like it.

You'd hear two of them talking sometimes , and one would say "I've been on a message longer than you've been here " and he'd be talking to a say 30 year man. But he'd have been there 40 odd years , been away , fought , survived and come back. That's the way they were at Levers.

We still realised though what a good job it was , when all the young lads went there, they'd never been outside. I'm talking about lads who had never gone looking around for a job from school. As long as your dad , or your cousin or someone worked in Levers , you got in, even at 15 years old. If you looked around you you'd see the same names coming up time after time , all the same families.

Later on , when I'd become steward , it was hard convincing the older men, who had never been anywhere else. They'd never seen their cards , been there 40 odd years and everyone knows them , ... us younger lads knew what a good job it was. So when the firm came along and said we have to be more competitive with the likes of Cadwalladers and firms like that , (they paid buttons and you slept in the cab and things like that) . I can still recall the meeting where the older lads were adamant that they weren't going to do any extra work. Of course they only had three or four years to go. The van lads were looking at another 20 or 30 years of work so were always willing to do more. Even the boss leaned toward the older lads point of view , he'd been there all that time with them all.

I remember the first time I went into the boss's office and slammed my hand down on his desk saying "I'm not having that "... whatever it was at the time. Well , you'd have thought I'd committed mass rape in the canteen , because there was absolute shock on his face , ...that seemed to say ... what right has he got to be here , he's only been here five minutes !!!

They were all moulded into the Lever way of things. One boss left after just eight months he said he couldn't take it anymore , those up above wouldn't let him get on with the job the way he thought it should be managed.

Norman Evans was the big boss and he had two team leaders who would take it upon themselves to dish out punishment, knocking half an hour off here , and half an hour there .When you came back into the yard you fuelled up, you would give your returns in, do your notes. If they spotted you in the yard around five o'clock, but you'd booked off at six o'clock. They'd book you off at half past five! Until I had to go in and sort it out , when I became steward . It took a little bit of power away from them. Norman wasn't a strong boss , but he was fair. But his boss , Gordon Sutcliffe , was the straightest boss I ever dealt with there union wise.

Phil Bramley was the main manager, he kidded me for years, and at the end of the day I didn't think he was a good guy.

When there was a National strike , 1981 or 1982 I think , me and Alan Jones our other union representative, went down to the union office and told the lads there that we could get into a fight for wages for outside contractors , but we couldn't vote , or do it with our feet , because we were already on twice what they were on anyway. So what we did was put our own picket on the gate, which was me and another lad. Anyone else that wanted to come in who were contractors, like Metal Box and the like , we made sure they had a written agreement to say that they were going to get the increase of , I think it was six percent then. The union was encouraging us to stop the vehicles going in, and Levers weren't too happy about that , but they were pleased that their stuff was still getting delivered by us. Believe it or not some of the staff , in the site warehouse , were calling us scabs because we would still be working.

Phil Bramley used to call down at the gate and bring us some soup and sandwiches from the canteen. We kept Levers going while everyone else shut down for eight weeks . I've always believed that if a man has never shit on you then you haven't got a beef . Phil Bramley, he never shitted on me until I left , and then he really showed his colours.

But Levers did everything in their power to keep the drivers happy. They kept me , Alan Jones and Billy Evans on 12 hours pay when we used to help out in the T&G offices. All our drivers kept working, they kept the place running. As long as we didn't do anything outside of what we usually did , no delivering to places that outside contractors would usually do.

It was the planners who would plan the loads . Long after that strike, there was one planner who, if you could be there 47 years, then he had been there that long. I often asked him why I could be delivering a load at say A, and just around the corner I'd see a contractor delivering Lever stuff too. I didn't seem to make sense. Until one day he was asked to go into the office about something and then he was given half an hour to clear his desk and go. The word was that he'd had his garden landscaped and all sorts as he'd been taking backhanders from outside firms to give them work.

Needless to say it was all very much played down at Levers... it never went further than a little rumble through the factory sort of thing.

Levers were always very safety conscious, I lost a finger in a Tescos in Liverpool, I had put a plate down, from the side of the wagon to the ground to pull the pallets off and slide them down, like a ramp, it was custom and practice. Of course, once this accident happened it was stated that this plate was only for the use of Tesco drivers, not other firms. Levers did the usual thing, they would assist me as much as they could as long as I didn't go for Levers. So they built a case up with me and the union solicitors, Benn & Twyford. Levers bent over backwards to give me anything I asked for, a day off to go here or there for tests and stuff. I never saw too many accidents but remember I was only there for a small part of each day. With the health and safety they tried their best.

We used to go to meetings in Kingston, lads like Eric Coates, Tony Patton and others. The T&G were always very reluctant to join in with anything else that was happening on the site with other unions like USDAW and such. Remember we'd be there with the chairman, office workers, the clerical staff. One guy, he was a lay preacher I think, said he didn't think it was right that the clerical staff should have to sit down with the drivers and talk, and he was supposed to be a man of the cloth! I can't remember exactly what I said to him but I almost shoved the words back down his throat! Looking back a lot of these Kingston meetings were just lip service really.

Really the drivers didn't want anything to do with it, but the firm was changing and they were bringing all these new wonder kids out of college, with their new outlook to life. Lots of new ones came in there, they'd introduce them as assistant manager this or that, there were that many come and go it was unbelievable, you just couldn't keep up with the names. So of course they wanted to come out on the wagons, and the drivers objected to that including me. It was just to see how long it takes, but at the end of the day you could kid them easily. You could go to say Stoke and pass the shop you were delivering to three or four times before they even knew it. They were looking for drivers who had finished at two o'clock and pulled into a lay-by.

They said they were looking at job improvement ,but we kept saying no. In the end they came back and said if we can look at your job for a month then you can come and look at this Personnel woman's job, she was called Sue something, we called her Thunderthighs. She'd come to break eggs with a big stick. She succeeded in many ways . She introduced the sick chart. They'd bring you in and show you the time you'd been off marked with red spots or no red spots. They tried to see lads without union representation, I believe that actually happens these days in Levers.

I agreed to do a fortnight in the end doing load planning. Then she'd say I'm doing this or that , for the afternoon , and I might go with her or not. She came out on the wagons with us but I just made sure I took the wrong route and if needed double backed on myself to justify the job. The new regime was just coming in then , from the directors down and even the managers were getting a good kick up the arse right left and centre too.

They succeeded in the end , they did change it all eventually.

We had fun times there too. We had one driver called Gomez , he was a Pakistani lad , I think he's driving taxis around Birkenhead now. Gomez was forever off or forever doing something wrong. He was a terrible lad for having Mondays and Fridays off.

He had family problems , divorced etc. Paying for his kids , living with another one and she'd thrown him out, but he just wasn't bothered. I was always going to disciplinaries with him , he had warning after warning after warning. One time I went up with him about the usual stuff, timekeeping etc. This time the manager was a guy called Reece , I think. There were so many , who all came and went.

As we went in he said " well Frank , that's it , we're going to sack him today. Look at his record .... this... and this... etc. etc. "

I went out to see Peter Gomez ... and he was so laid back.... I said Peter , it doesn't look too good this time Peter... they want to sack you this time.
He just said , rolling himself a fag , "you just do the talking for me Birksie, man."

So we went in and Sutcliffe, the big boss, was there too. Sutcliffe went around and around and basically said he was being sacked.
Gomez just said " I'd like my representative to speak for me man. "

Remember that Gomez had no idea what I was going to say , neither did I really.

So I told this tale how he'd been living. Wife , divorce , paying for kids , thrown out by another one and ended up by saying that for the last week he'd been sleeping in Birkenhead Park and that every time he'd tried to get a flat , he'd see vacancy signs , but because he was a black man , they'd suddenly run out of vacancies.

They were horrified. I'd actually said the words "black man " and this highly embarrassed them. Gomez was just nodding his head and rolling another fag , tapping his fag on his tin , and nodding his head.

Sutcliffe got up and said " my god man , why didn't you tell us ? Why didn't you come to us ? Would you like a coffee ? "

So he arranged coffees and then disappeared for a while. When he came back he gave Gomez a phone number and explained that this was one of Levers contacts who had six flats available , and Gomez could pick the one he wanted.

So he'd gone in , lined up for the sack and come out with a coffee and the choice of six flats.

As we were walking back he said to me "Birksie , you did really well for me there , yes you did , but how are you going to sort out this problem now ?"

I said " I just have , you cheeky bastard. What's wrong with that ?"

He said , " Yes , but now I'm paying for the wife and kids place , I'm paying for the other ones' flat , and now can you tell me how I'm going to pay for another flat ? "

Sometimes , you just can't win.

What I think really killed off the fleet was when some of the drivers were all caught robbing gear. I was on holiday at the time and got a call from a manager, through his secretary, could we meet and have lunch ? He showed me a statement from some unnamed source that various drivers and warehouse men were taking and selling Levers gear.

I thought it was just Levers after some guys for taking a few bars of soap, but he said no , it's a bit more than that, we're talking about whole pallets of gear here.

I said it was too big for me and a full-time official should deal with it. That was really the beginning of the end for the van fleet in my opinion.

I ended up meeting some lads at night , near Lairds main gate, as they prepared their case as they were pulled in one by one.

I was usually at these meetings, and they had a thing in Levers that they called "coats off" which meant everything said was unofficial and off the record between me and the manager concerned. I asked if what they were offering was if a driver goes for "personal reasons" that would be that.

The reply was "in a nutshell yes."

So that's the way it went, with a number of drivers one at a time. One lad asked me about his house on the village, would he lose it? The deal was no, that he wouldn't.

To make the decision to leave was hard. I knew that they would do to me in the end when they went to contract vehicles used in total, and finished up the van fleet. They would either tap me on the head and say well O.K. Frank, you've been a good lad, get yourself over there on that stacker truck and unload those wagons, or go into an office and do whatever. Or they'd put me on a shitty job.

They put me on a shitty job, in the Pears, a terrible place. I was only there four days before I went to see the boss to try and get out.

Now, I'm still in contact with a lot of people there, and they say it's horrible, you can't look at the boss, you can't do this, you can't do that. But these are in the main long time Lever people who've been there all their lives. They've never worked in a say a little tanyard, downtown. But I'd go back tomorrow if my legs were in better shape. Just to drive a van. I miss it very much indeed.

Richard Godwin

D.O.B 25.12.22

Production Planner

Worked in Levers
1940-1984

I was only a lad of 18 . I actually started work at the Cotton Exchange in Liverpool on September 4th 1939, which was the day after the war broke out. I was there until April 1940. I finished work at the Cotton Exchange on the Saturday and started at Levers on the Monday. I left the Cotton Exchange because the trip to and from Liverpool, which I did through the tunnel on a push bike, was getting me down and one day when I looked around the office there and saw these little wizened old men sitting on these tall stools at Victorian desks and thought "My God this could be me one day". I remembered I'd been round Levers, probably in l936 or 37 and I'd been impressed. I remembered this and wrote in, got an application form and attended for interview.

I remember the first day. I arrived at the vestibule and then went into the East Wing, into the first office, up a couple of steps and into the area in front of the office where the secretary sat, Mary Kirby, I still see her around. She was the Personnel Supervisor's Secretary and also Secretary to the Personnel Manager, Mr Watson. I saw him and he took some extra details and a photograph and then he took me along to the Traffic Department in the South Wing and introduced me to Taff Davies, the supervisor, who showed me to a particular desk and introduced me to one or two other people.

This was, of course in the days before computers, and the wing was quite a large rectangular office with an upper balcony where the Directors were located. Down below on each side you had the Managers offices with an office in front of the Manager's office, where the secretary sat. There was a passageway which went right around with a mahogany screen and in the middle were the staff, supervisors, clerks and typing pool and the various departments were in blocks. There were about maybe five or six desks which ran right down the room. Each one had a curved chrome tube and a green glass lampshade, it looked very impressive. My desk was at the front and someone came along and gave me an outline of the type of work I'd be doing and took me around one or two places in the factory which pretty much took up most of the first day.

I was a little apprehensive because it was a big place, there were a hell of a lot of people and nothing like I'd been used to before. The factory was nothing whatsoever like the factory is today. At that time, war-time, there were about 9,500 people, before the war there'd probably been about 14,000, now it's less than 1,500. Everything was moved by rail, there were one or two vehicles with trailers used on internal movements, but raw materials came in by water i.e. Bromborough Dock or wherever, barges into the wharf, then from the wharf, derricked up into the hard standing there and stored and then moved in to the melting out stage or wherever. Mostly they were drums or cylinders of oil, barrels of resin. They were mostly barrels. There were one or two tankers.

I went their because there was better money too. There was more money but also because there was more opportunity and such a variety of work. The first job I had was a statistical job which bored me rigid, it would never happen now because it would all be done by computer but in those days it was gathering in statistics on materials coming in to and going out of the factory, this was in big ledgers. I did that for about 12 months.

I was a Clerical Assistant. I then indicated I was interested in looking at other facets of the business so I was still within Traffic Department, ruled over by a man named George Bertie Lissenden, and he was an absolute swine, a bully. He was the Traffic Controller with an office on the balcony which automatically meant that he was next to God. He wore Stetson hats, usually green, people walked in fear of him. He was a total bully.

During the 12 months I was in the South Wing I had a week's holiday and a girl took over my job. When I came back I was called into his office, I didn't know what the hell for, and he proceeded to wipe the floor with me because the statistics were totally wrong. He went rattling on and when I tried to explain that I hadn't compiled the figures as I'd been off he wanted to know who had compiled the figures. When I suggested he had a word with the supervisor he said "never mind the

Supervisor, who compiled those figures?". When I told him I thought Miss Randle had done them he told me to get her up to the office. Miss Randle came up and he wiped the floor with the poor girl who was in floods of tears. He was a nasty piece of work.

I then moved down to River Traffic which was located in an office on the wharf. There were two offices next to one another, one was the Stevedores and the other was occupied by Seth Evans who was Supervisor over barge movements. At that time we had a fleet of barges, they were mostly steam powered, we had two diesel barges. On one of them the engine was manufactured by Primus and they were peculiar engines. To start them there was a flywheel which had a number of slots into which you fitted a bar and swung the fly wheel over up to compression and then put the bar in again and took it up to compression as far as it would go and whipped the bar out quick. It was a two cylinder device and if I remember rightly it was a hot bulb ignition. Before you started up you had to set up four blow lamps and there was a bulb on each cylinder head and you fired two blow lamps on each of these bulbs and they just operated until the bulbs were virtually red hot and that's when you swung it over. Once you'd got it started you could turn the blow lamps off.

I was dealing with a movement of these tankers which operated between Bromborough Dock, all the docks in Liverpool and Birkenhead, Eastham Locks, Upton Lay-by and Manchester Docks, Some of the barges you wouldn't see for two or three weeks and this was wartime and they were on special rations because they went all over the place. We also had about 50 other barges.

After the war when I came back I was in No.1 Soapery which at that time was Liquids and Hard Soaps. At that time the supervisor in COS. Dept., Control of Supplies, was a bloke named Cooper. These were the materials used for packing soap, wrappers, greaseproof layers, stiffeners, whatever was used in packaging. We also had bottles for Handy Andy, Sunlight liquid, Lux liquid etc. The Supervisor, Cooper, was as thick as two short planks, totally out of his depth - he'd been George Bertie Lissenden's chauffeur and he used to take Lissenden, after hours, to his various speaking engagements, as Lissenden was a bit of an author. He even used to take him home and help Mrs Lissenden wash the dishes up.

Anyway, Lissenden, as payment if you like, made him a supervisor in Traffic Department, Transport. He was useless. What would happen was you'd order in transport from the Dept. to do a movement of material and the vehicle would arrive at the stage, you'd get hold of the storekeeper to let him know that the wagon was ready to load, the storekeeper would get the stuff ready to load, get it down to the loading stage, and the vehicle had gone. Cooper had come along, spotted the vehicle and sent it somewhere else, without contacting anybody. People got fed up with this and got hold of the Commercial Director and he told the Head of COS., Stan Wood, that he would have to find this fella, Cooper, a job. He was totally useless. It got to the stage when I threatened to wrap a desk round his neck.

After that he kept out of my way. The only time he got involved with anything was when I was in the Army Reserve and I used to do a fortnights camp each year. When I got back from the camp I was looking through the mail on my desk and I'd left Cooper a load of files, told him what to put where and who to contact if he was in any difficulty. I was going through the paperwork and said "What did you do with this one?" and he said "I thought I'd leave that until you got back". I said "Well, this is for cancelling a product promotion, we've got 20,000 fibroid cases laid down for this. Did you do anything about this?"
"No."
I got hold of Buying Department and asked if they could cancel it, but they couldn't, so I got hold of Cooper and told him there would be trouble over this one. He told me he thought the letter had come in before I went off, but the letter was dated the Monday after I went off on the Friday. A real cock-up that was.

At one stage when I was in the Army, in India, I wondered if I could make a career of it, but I came home on leave after three and a half years , then went back and decided to leave the Army after the war. After I'd got back from the Army service they had to take you back. They offered me two jobs. One was in the Baby Food Dept. and the other was in the Estate Dept. so I opted for the Estate Department. I was there for four years. That was an interesting job. There was a certain amount of detailed drawing which I was doing, and some surveying. I was also finding accommodation in the graveyard because they were running short of space. I found room for l00 which wasn't bad going. You have to be careful because sometimes you can only go two deep because of the water table, because the creek used to flow at the back of the graveyard.

What was even more interesting was that when I left I was getting perhaps a couple of quid a week and when I came back I was getting four pound ten shillings a week, which was pretty fair wages. So I did four years in the Estate Dept. and there were prospects in the factory in Civil Engineering so I put in for a Technical Clerk's job. I got this particular job but unfortunately the work that I as doing was gradually moved to the main Civil engineering office and other people started to get the work I'd been doing so I was left with the dregs. In the end I got a bit fed up and said I'd like to try something else. I got an interview for a job in the COS. Dept. and I was there for about three years.

A supervisor's job came up so I went for it but I didn't get it although I was runner-up. I applied for another job and got short-listed and eventually got the job of supervisor in COS. Dept. Toilet Soaps which was a more complex job than anything I'd done previously. I did two or three years of that and moved on to NSD - Non Soap and Detergent, like Omo or Persil, and that was a different type of job. They call it non-soap because there's no soap in them. None at all . The last soap powder made here was Rinso, before the war. The place where Rinso was made was bombed during the war and when the sprinkler system went off the firemen were waist high in soap suds.

I eventually became a Deputy Divisional Manager on toilet soaps. I took over from the supervisor on Detergents and the supervisor on the Planning side of NSD moved on and I took over the two supervisors jobs. It was probably the best job I'd had there. It was the best and the worst. It was the best insofar as there was an infinite variety of work. You couldn't determine what you were going to do each day because you were involved in problem solving, new situations arising, cancellations, everything had to be coped with. I did that job for maybe three years. Then there was a vacancy for Assistant Planning Manager - he controlled the Toilet Soap side. I was one of six nominees and I got the job, I took over from Arthur Evans.

There were three Assistant Managers, me, Peter Holmes and Frank Burns. Then there was a reorganisation at Head Office in London and they had a spare manager. I was told that the position that I held was going to become a full management position and they already had a manager who would be doing my job. I was not best pleased. This bloke knew nothing at all about Planning. I had to keep the job going for six months until he arrived. I had to show him the ropes - for the first twelve months he was not a lot of use. My main efforts were to try and keep him out of trouble and try and instil into him the gentle art of Production Planning which in those days, of course, with no computerisation, was done the hard way.

You had to plan for 12 months and every month you had to reestablish the next 12 month production, things changed all the while because of competition from Procter and Gamble, Colgate Palmolive and our own competition in reply to that so you'd have to recast the whole thing. The first three months were done in detail, weekly detail and the remainder was done in four week cycles. After two years this bloke was pulling his weight and then he got posted and another one arrived. What happened was that this became a position for trainees, people who came into Unilever as management trainees, did their initial training and got their first position and this was designated one of those training type slots. Over the next few years I trained seven of them, some of them lasted one year, some lasted two. Sometimes there was a hand-over between one and his successor, sometimes there was a gap in which case I carried the can. If anything went wrong I'd get the blame for not training the person properly. Nevertheless I liked the job, I enjoyed it. It was hectic, I usually got into the office at about 7.15 a.m. and got away at about 6.00 p.m.

The worst job I ever had in Levers was probably in the Civil Engineering. There didn't seem to be anything on the horizon. You'd keep your eye on the notice board to see what jobs were coming up but there didn't seem to be anything. There were two or three managers in Civil Engineering when I was there - Acres was the first, Jim Anderson, a very nice bloke and he was followed by Sanchez .He worked, before the War in the Estate office at Thornton Hough, the private estate of Lord Leverhulme and he was well qualified, he was a major in the Engineers during the war and he came back to the Civil Engineering Section of the Estate Dept. and then he went to the Factory as Civil Engineering Manager.

I didn't like some of my bosses in those days ,and there was more than one.

A large company can survive an awful lot of idiots. They can be swallowed and hidden.

Some of them were good though. It depends. Some are better at some things than others. Kim Cartlidge was one of the best. She was pretty good, she wasn't afraid to make waves. I wasn't the only awkward bugger around though , far from it. I just stuck to my views. If I thought I was right then I was not going to change. I usually won.

I remember I had one or two run-ins with the Production Manager on NSD, Frank Harris. You were in an awkward position, you couldn't order the Production Dept. to do anything. You were responsible for what they produced so you had to have the right approach. It was a very fine relationship which was built up. The worst thing was when the Production Manager changed and you had to start again. I remember having a bit of an argument with Frank Harris over some aspect of planning, I forget what it was. He came into the office, late on in the day and I said "Look, you think Planning is easy - let's have a little test". I had an idiot board, it was a piece of board covered with a grid with a sheet of acetate over it and I could create a pattern of columns and if I wanted to try and do an alteration to a plan, I wrote down a few things and said "Look, we've got to try and produce a few things, here's the situation".

I gave him the pencils and the idiot board. He probably took half an hour and when he'd finished I got a red pencil and put bloody big red circles on it, and told him which would work and which wouldn't and why. After I'd gone through several of these he admitted there was more to planning and that was fair enough.

Later on we were occupying the same office in the Terrapin building, which was a temporary building and he had an office created in the corner. I remember this particular day, he'd been losing weight and my office was in the opposite corner. Anyway Frank Harris came back from his lunch and behind his desk was a card on the wall and there was a potato crisp sellotaped on it and underneath "For Emergency Use Only". He came straight down the office, stood in front of my desk and said "You bastard". He finished up as Factory Manager in Torquay the last I heard.

There were some accidents, I recall , some were bad ones. There was a painter who got his legs mangled in a railway accident. In those days there was a lot of railway traffic and normally you didn't cross the railway lines. There were sub-ways - if you were going into the No. 3 Soapery there were sub-ways under the road. This was to avoid the inter-sections of the railway lines. Then there was Harry Rule. He was a draftsman, worked in the engineering office. There was a blowing tower in the Printing Dept. which was walled off. That was for industrial detergents and occasionally I used to blow powder down that tower to supplement the other two towers. It was quite high and I had the job of measuring up the roof and the angles. Harry Rule went off the top of the tower and he hit the roof. He wasn't killed but he had serious head injuries. There was no mention of it anywhere.

We had medical staff though. We started off with a surgery in every Soapery and then there was a central one. Then they were all joined into one and a new modern building was created. They had

Physiotherapy, Doctors, Dentist, Opticians. They were very good. Sister Campbell was the Senior Nurse.

In the early days I remember a tale about the Wisk. It was the first detergent we ever did and it was produced in a blowing tower which was located in the bottom end of No. 3 and it was one of those things which probably had too high a moisture content. What happens is very high pressure pumps the slurry up the tower and it comes out through a ring main at the top, through specially designed nozzles, it doesn't drop down the tower it swirls. It's a drying tower basically. In this swirling process it makes the time to get from the top of the tower to the bottom that much longer, that much more drying time. This was the first tower designed and used and quite obviously they hadn't got the technology quite right, this was in the fifties sometime I think. Basically the stuff set like concrete. It didn't work. It never hit the market. It happens in all industries.

There were things like Dove, you see Dove advertised on T.V. This is the third time we've produced Dove. What happens normally is that they produce it, it goes into a test market and then if the assessment of the test market is OK then they go national. A test market is usually a television region and they push the advertising in that area, evaluate it and see how it sells and then make their decision. Sometimes they don't get any further than test market and they die the death. Sometimes, they go national. Lyrol was one that went national but didn't last long before they dropped it. You could have a bloody good product and for whatever reason it doesn't go. It's probably ahead of its time.

Like Presto tablets, these are compressed tablets of detergent. Instead of dosing a powder in you just put a tablet in, but we got all this ready, we had the whole production area set up, the machines were there and we were waiting to see if the opposition went, Procter and Gamble, and they didn't go, so we didn't go. There was no point in getting into a war we didn't have to. It's like that with machines. Before the war all the toilet soaps were hand wrapped, so if you wanted a lot of soap you had to have a lot of girls. They were marvellous at it. Then they started to get machines in and these were producing 300 tablets a minute and we had a machine delivered here for a trial which was capable of producing 400 bars a minute.

They had the machine delivered, stripped the case off, ready to go in, they wanted to take the ACME machine out and put this one in. I wouldn't let them because I couldn't spare the capacity. I was going to lose a month's production from the ACME machine while they installed this machine and then it would take a month to get it going. What they did was repacked it and sent it off to Germany. We've had machines here that have still had plenty of life in them but they had been superseded by later models with a greater capacity, higher speed, better quality product.

I'd do a few things differently but I'd work there again. There are a lot worse places than there. I keep getting this vision of the Cotton Exchange and I'd think of that and think "Thank Christ I'm at Levers."

I was married when I was about 30, we both worked together in the Estate office. I stayed so long I think because, well, I couldn't think of anywhere better to go and the point is the work I was doing was so specialised that my skills here were probably almost unique to this place, but I enjoyed what I was doing on the Planning side. I couldn't think of anywhere with the same sort of pace. I was living in the village and I would have to have left and bought a house. I still live here in this Lever house.

It's been good fun, had a lot of laughs, some grim moments. When I was in the Estate Department a chap joined as a labourer and in those days there was a two or three day induction course, training in the factory, talking about soap making, how Levers started, the size of the Unilever organisation etc. Then he went down to the Estate Dept. and they put him on digging graves - he'd never dug a grave in his life. He got down to the top coffin, there were already two there and he went through both coffins. I think he made it out of the grave in one jump - he never went back. I remember another lad who always used to finish on time, he was based in the joiners shop. If he was doing a job outside he'd have his tool boxes with him and on this particular day he'd locked his tool box up. He went to pick it up, got hold of the handle, and he nearly pulled his shoulder out. It had been screwed to the deck, some swine had put three inch screws through the bottom of his tool box, straight through the floor. He must have spent about half an hour trying to get those screws out.

I'm glad I got out though. Everybody who I've met who retired about the same time as me are glad they got out. The people who are left now are not very happy. When I worked there we were satisfied that we had job security. Now, I've met several batches of people who've been required to leave either voluntarily or whatever. People don't really know how long they've got a job for, what new technical innovation is going to appear which will make their job obsolete. Computers and new technology mean that lots of jobs which were done manually are now computerised.

There's no more paternalism. That doesn't exist now, it did do. It was very strong indeed. It all changed. It happened because policy used to be formed here, it's no longer formed here, it's now formed at Kingston Head office and the people down there. To them Sunlight is out of sight. The accountants have come to the fore. Everything now relates to the bottom line. They won't spend money unless they get a substantial return. For example, with the village. They used to maintain a labour force of several hundred people at the Estate Yard, every building trade, to maintain the properties in the village. Gradually they cut back and then closed everything down. They work on the principle that (a) you've bought your house so they're not concerned about it or (b) you're a tenant. If you're a tenant you're going to die anyway so therefore let's leave things as they are and whoever buys the house can do any repairs required.

Old Billy Lever though was ahead of his time. He created the factory.
He's dossed down in the churchyard there. When we get visitors round here and they talk about the village I say to them "Have you been to the Art Gallery?"
"Oh yes",
"Have you been down to the Church?"
"No, not yet".

I tell them that the best time to go down to the church is on a cool, quiet summer evening, look on the left hand side of the church entrance for the little notice which says Founder's Tomb. Billy Lever is dossed down there. If you listen very carefully you'll hear a humming sound like a turbine, as you get closer the whining , humming noise gets a little louder , and a little louder - that's old Billy Lever spinning in his grave because of what they've done to his factory. I reckon if they wired him up he could keep this village going on electricity.

When he created this lot, you were still in the dark satanic mills era. Life was grim in factories then, but he created this village for the workers. The houses at the top end of the road here on the left hand side, they were the first houses built in the village. They were two up two down - the village was going to look like that, then he changed his mind for whatever reason. The village actually never finished up as he originally designed it, because he kept changing his mind and on a lot of the open spaces houses were going to be built ,but I think he warmed to the idea of the open spaces and also there were three estates, the

Bromborough one and the Woodhead estate. If you look at those houses they're very similar to the Sunlight houses. They were sold in the 1950's to the sitting tenants. He didn't need any more houses because some of those houses were empty and he let them to people who didn't work at Levers.

I'm finished now, I keep busy with my garden and making tubs and gates and the like. I do the frontage, and there's a prize for the most colourful frontage. I've won it six times out of the last seven years. The last four years has been an all expenses paid trip to the Chelsea Flower show.

I'm a Lever pensioner now, and they could try to do more things for the pensioners , but they don't. They could do it better. They used to have a Liaison officer who used to keep in touch with the pensioners but there's nothing like that now. There's not even any shops any more for us, just the place around the corner where they let you have cheap soap. There used to be shops over the road, butchers, drapers, grocers. The shops that were here before the war got bombed. They supplied the village but anybody went in. When they were bombed they took over the gymnasium which was next to the Baths, then it became the Boys Club, then it was demolished and the baths filled in.

It's sad we've lost the baths, the gymnasium, the auditorium, bandstand. These things have gone and will never be replaced.

Levers Main Entrance circa 1931. It could be an ice cream stand on the left.

Elspeth Campbell
D.O.B 7.9.36

Occupational Health Nurse

Worked in Levers 1965-present

My first job was for Unilever. On my first official day, I left the United Kingdom, with great difficulty because in those days BOAC was the airline that was flying international. I went to leave the international airport, as it was then known in London, and it was snowed up. It took four hours for them to get the snow off the wings of the aircraft. Eventually we took off going from London to Akrah, Nigeria. When we arrived in Akrah I had actually organised an evening engagement with a mutual friend, at Legon University in Akrah, for dinner with a friend. Unfortunately, as we had arrived at 10 o'clock at night, that was off and I was taken almost immediately to the rest house as it was called. So my first official working day I spent travelling.

The following day I had to arrange my registration, although we had reciprocal registration arrangements, it was still necessary to register in Akrah with the registration authority there. I was taken round and registered as both a Nurse and Midwife. Then I went from Akrah to Takoradi, by plane, the kind you wound up with elastic in those days but it went up and it came down again thank God. I stayed overnight in Takoradi, before going onto the plant of African Timber and Plywood, which was part of the United Africa Company in those days. It's ceased production for UAC nowadays, but that was my first job, as matron of a hospital for a plywood factory in Africa.

I pretty much knew what to expect, as my uncle who was a town clerk of Akrah prior to me going out there, used to come home and had told me about the type of life there in West Africa, so I wasn't totally blinkered about the life in Africa . I'd done my tropical diseases at Liverpool so I had little bit of experience in this field.

I had mostly responsibility for out and in patients, we had a maternity unit and I was in charge of the public health within a defined area for the company people and some local people in the bush, because we did timber extractions' as well as processing for the company. Out there, were multi-national workers on the management side as well as Nigerian and Ghanaian workers in the factories there, and we had to treat them all with primary health care. The company had its own ambulance and everything came to us first .

I had reached the stage in nursing were I could either progress to administrative work or teaching. I didn't like or want to do either of those things . I wanted to work in the clinical field. I have I suppose achieved that as I still remain in the clinical field today . I had come to believe that as a nurse it was my duty and part of the job to be caring for the actual patient , if they be ill or fit, it's part of nursing . Teaching or admin. just never appealed to me as a full time job. I still do a bit of teaching here and there.

I wanted experience of overseas work ,which I don't regret at all. I think it gives you a different culture, a different view of life. More tolerance of people and an understanding of the multi-cultural society. I thought the company looked after its people very well indeed. The company was quite big in West Africa in those days. They had built houses, they had their own power station , we purified our own water, we had a filtration system and primary health care. Piped water to all the villages was quite something in those days. To have a source of fresh water for good clean drinking was in some ways better than they have in parts of Africa today. We didn't have the terrible outbreaks of diseases like Cholera and Typhoid that you see in some of these camps in war-torn Africa today, simply because of good drinking water.

I returned after two and a half years of being in Africa, as was employed by Bachelors Foods Ltd., in Sheffield. We were the pea kings in those days, we did frozen peas, we did dried peas, we did canned peas and I never looked at peas for a good few years after that , I just couldn't take them. It was an interesting job in a food processing plant. They had a head office and some other factories , but the only one that survives today is the factory at Worksop.

In 1971 the position of Nursing Superintendent arose. It was to be based in the health center here at Port Sunlight. This position was the most senior nursing job that you could have , apart from the Principal

Nursing Advisor at Unilever House, within Unilever. I applied for it and , fortunately or unfortunately , I got the job. I stayed there until in December 1989, when Lever Brothers , in their infinite wisdom decided they no longer wished to use UML Services . In those days Unilever Management Ltd. , UML, provided all the services to all the Unilever companies on site. Unilever then decided that they wanted their own nursing staff and the X-ray girl. I was put out to grass at Research and that's where I am at the moment.

Of all the duties that I had to do, I least enjoyed disciplining of staff . It would have to be the worst job I had to do because it took so much out of you. I never, ever took any pleasure in disciplining them and I still don't to this day. However, I don't do as much of it now as I haven't got the staff to do so.

The job that I liked doing the most was putting on a dressing that I knew would stay on. I knew it would be comfortable for the patient and I could attend and give the best treatment and watch over the injury until it was healed. I could start primary health treatment and see it right through to the end. Now we do less and less, as there is less mechanisation. Over the years the statistics for accidents has gone down, of course the workforce is much reduced too. We still get the odd nasty one , but I can remember when we used to get people coming in with terrible burns. We had a fleet at one time the tankers coming into Liverpool, and we took part loads of oil over to into Sunlight, and some of the accidents on the boats were really not very pleasant. We used to get the African boats in the docks too then. Now of course the whole fleet and the whole port is closed. I found the clinical aspect of my job most rewarding. From start to finish I was a Clinical Practitioner.

We had all sorts of accidents. At one time in Lever Bros., we had a lot of nasty eye accidents. The stuff they put in powders, especially powders , they no longer make powders here today , especially mercury, would get into their eyes. I remember two men , one has just died , who had this. I also had one person , an assistant manager ,who got sulphuric or sulphonic acid, I can't remember which , into his eyes. He was given a corneal graft over at St. Pauls in Liverpool , as it was then ,but it didn't take and his eyesight was never the same. He's since died.

Some were operators , but the other two were engineers, clearing out tanks and things .We did many many eye injuries, we had a standard procedure. I found it very rewarding to deal with some nasty eyes , you had the skills and the procedure to be able to treat them and improve them. Eyes were very common. As were hands and feet , because hands and feet are always getting in the way of things. Burns were common too, especially from the old soapmaking processes, from the pan room. We'd get splashes of hot boiling soap. It was both a hot burn and it was a chemical burn, some were very nasty.

I can't really say much about best boss or bad bosses, as professionally I was responsible to people managerially. But I was professionally responsible for myself, I would be appraised every year, the same as everyone else. Some liked my attitude to my work more than others but they were all professional in the way they would go about the appraisals. I could never say that I was unfairly treated or unfairly appraised, because I never was. They were very fair with me. If I had had a particularly bad year, then I had a bad year. We don't go along in life being wonderful all the time. Like everybody else I had some good years and some bad years . If I had a good year they would say so, they were equally as good as bosses. If we had a problem they'd help you solve them, if you drifted downwards they would tell you so. If you had a super or smashing year they'd say , well done.

The best part of working here for me has been the scope of experience and the different aspects of the different companies and the experience. It is purely research now. That just used to be an element before, now they are all mine as the saying goes . We had the nitty gritty of the man on the shop floor, and I hate to say it , a lot of youngsters in those days , which I miss very much. We're not taking on young people now , unfortunately. We used to get apprentices in by the ton, they used to drive me bananas but I miss it now, bless them . There were youngsters on the colour mix and every Christmas I would go around and would warn them that drunkeness was not an occupational hazard and to be careful on the production line. In those days, Lux soap was available in many colours. Today you can just have pink or white. It was mixed in boxes, blue, yellow, pink, green , whatever. We had youngster standing on the line putting three of each colour into boxes, hence the colour mix. It was dreadful job and they would all have done anything to get off it. That had its problems with hands and joints too. Nowadays you'd call it RSI. Repetitive Strain Injury.

We had the engineers too who were a high risk, they could be a problem as they had to test things , and fingers get in the road and that. The engineers were always problem children.

In those days we were dealing with occupational problems of dust and enzymatic powders. As well as that we had BOCM too , all the animal feeds stuff , and that had some nasty ones as well. The pinging pellets as I recall them, they'd come out at speed and hit the metal chutes and the noise level was very high , they dosed some of the feeds with chemicals too.

Like most people I always remember the good times , and not the bad times. I think towards the end of my service there , some of the companies became very demanding, and although you tried to please them it became difficult to please any of the people any of the time. It became very frustrating. They wanted their people seen first , it was a case of trying to keep all the balls in the air. You tried to please them all but you couldn't and it was very frustrating. You knew that you were doing your best but the best wasn't good enough. Their people had to be seen first if they were injured and it was impossible for you to keep all the companies happy.

We did an awful lot of screening too. All the new entrants were screened , we reviewed all the enzyme workers, if we sent people overseas, we did the vaccinations and immunisations, we tested the stacker truck drivers, that's a lot of work. We still do, even more so with the European laws. But we had to organise our time schedule so that we saw one company on one specific day and another company on a different day so that we could please them all. But they always wanted to switch it or whatever, it was difficult.

At one time, it's much less active now, but at one time the unions were quite powerful and had many more members. The engineering unions were quite powerful . I think it was around 1975-1985, during those ten years that , because of the union action, the company had to cease putting enzymes into the powders. The unions did not want their members to be exposed to this substance. At the end of that time , because of the market loss that the company had suffered , they entered into negotiations again with the unions.

There was a breadth of unions then, the T&G were active, USDAW was active, ASTMS was active. There was even a sailmaker, and he was in his own special union. I can see him yet ,Old Smith the sailmaker . I can remember when the idea of a management union was first mooted. This was totally new to me , to be a member of a union, because my great problem was that despite the fact that I liked their advice and their backing on industrial situations, I never wished to be in the position where I would be asked to withdraw my labour. My nursing staff were in ASTMS at the time and at one time they were put in a very difficult position because they were asked to withdraw their labour. But they asked for an exemption clause because in their heart of hearts they didn't professionally wish to leave their work.

At one time it was very very strong , you could hardly move without talking to the unions , but it wasn't our unions that I remember having such a big impact, it was the time when Merseyside Fire Service went on strike and our No. Three Soapery went up. We had the Green Goddess's in and they dealt with the fire. I had a report waiting for me from my night nurse . I remember it said "Commander in Chief reports all fires extinguished , Army leaving site."

You have to know the people. If you have a normally very garrulous man who comes in and is very quiet , you know there is something amiss, and the same the other way round. We had some mental illnesses too. I'm not anti engineers , but I got to know a lot of engineers. But they still do it to this day. They tend to cover up for their pals , they won't split on their pals. If someone had say an epileptic fit , they'd maybe get him in a corner until he comes around . It was only if they failed to get him round that someone, whoever , Joe Bloggs would let the cat out of the bag. They just didn't want anyone to know. They didn't want to tell me. Or if someone had been on the pop, they'd cover up for him , or do his shift until he was sobered up , in case he might lose his job. Because the fear of job loss , even in those days , was very high. Today it's even higher, as in all industries.

I see no reason why I wouldn't do it again except with my knowledge now I would probably have tried to become better educated, gone to University, I think , because today's high flyers all have a University background. It's the basic element required now, to get a University degree. I wasn't in my day but is more so today. Even nursing now is going to need a University degree.

In 1986, the principal Nursing Advisor Unilever retired , and that post was not replaced in those days. So I was as high as you could go, in my field , in Unilever. So you either left Unilever to get something outside, or stayed. I really didn't want to go anywhere else. I'd reached a plateau, perhaps it was too comfortable a plateau, maybe I might have done better moving on, but I didn't and I don't really regret it. Occupational Health is not on the upward trend , quite the reverse. Many Occupational Health Advisors that were, are no longer, no longer in post. And by that time my brain would probably not have taken going and doing any further training.

We go on training courses now of course , but if I've done nothing else here I've helped train a lot of nurses towards their Occupational Health certificates and the like. They all hold certificates and can actually work independently without mummy holding their hands.

The company today is less paternalistic than it was once , 30 years ago. It cannot carry dead wood. It's working in a different world now. We all are. But if I were a young woman again today I wouldn't go through it again now. This is shrinking, the breadth is no longer here. Industry is shrinking , I don't think I'd even do nursing if I was 29 years old again today , I think I'd be thinking about further education , perhaps a University degree . In which direction I'd go I just don't really know.

Bill Smith
D.O.B 15.8.15

Process Operator
Worked in Levers
1937-1978
(Five year break as a
Prisoner of war)

I was a young lad of 18 when I started. I remember my first day very well. I was late, in those days I was a keen cyclist. Levers had a big shed for all cycles but I wasn't sure what was to happen so I thought that I would get the bus for that particular morning. I lived in Clover Street then, and the bus used to come up at half past five, I was on six-to-two. Well, I thought I had plenty of time so I walked up and as I reached the top of Victoria Road the bus sailed past the top of Victoria. So I ran all the way behind the bus, I was a keen athlete then. I didn't know all the ropes then at Sunlight, and if you were late you had to report to the gateman, but instead of doing so all I could think of doing was getting through the gates and getting down to number four Soapery.

The first person I should meet up with was the Supervisor, well a foreman then, I had told this particular supervisor in an interview that I was quite good at getting up , being a shift worker all my life, particularly as I was a milk lad at the age of 14 and I was up at 4 o'clock in the morning. Then I got finished there because I was 16 and at that age your employer had to pay insurance for you. I then got a job in the flour mills, during the depression from the 1930s, I managed to get this job in the mills through this aunt who already worked there. The depression deepened and everything went, all the young people like me were finished up and the older chaps kept on. In them days it is not like it is today, so I was a bit disappointed at it and I do reminisce sometimes about it how I came to get to Levers .

Heseltine said "Get on your bike" didn't he. Well in those days I used to cycle all around the factories, BOC, Stork, all over , looking for a job. I was in the T.A. then, and as it happened , my C.O. worked at Sunlight, . I used to see him coming in every morning.

"Morning Sir " says I.

"Morning Smith " he'd say.

This went on for a few weeks. Then I heard that there was a re-organisation in number four Soapery, it was making Rinso then . They were going onto relay work, well the girls were not allowed to work relay work . So they needed some men for that job. Then half way through the week they changed it over to three shifts , so it was pretty hectic then.

What I really expected on my first day was to get the sack after being late. I had heard that many stories about it, the foreman's word was law and it was only the fact that I was a footballer and the supervisor/ foreman who caught me, George Tasker, he was the Chairman of Port Sunlight Football Club, did a little bit of "wheeling and dealing". I didn't play for Sunlight, I played for Vernon's Flour Mills, my old firm and also Thorndale, we shared the same ground in the social club in Wallasey.

I started there during the depression and jobs were very hard to come by. I had come to the end of my tether. I was in the T.A., I'd done my basic training, but that was that. I had said to my father, who was also my Sergeant Major, that if I didn't get a job this week I would join the army. It was a good thing for a young man in those days , you got your pay, clothing etc.

Then one morning my old boss , the C.O.went past me. It was the usual thing,

"Morning Sir ."

"Morning Smith."

Then he turned round and asked what number Clover Street did I live at and I told him. Off he went and I never thought anything more of it . I went home and was getting ready upstairs to go to a matinee at the old Empire, to pass the afternoons away. Then I heard a knock at the door and a voice said "Does a Mr William Smith live here?"

"Yes" said my mother.

"Report to the Health Centre for two o'clock." And that was it.

I said to my dad " Bloody Hell , he would have to come now, wouldn't he, and I really wanted to see that picture ! "

I used to think it was a good company when I was younger, but now that they have changed the name of the company from Lever Brothers to Unilever, I detest that name. The people who I worked with were very helpful to one another, worked for one another, it was comradeship. They were all a happy bunch, they would talk to one another. It is not like today when it's all machinery, like a robot that does the work. In them days the workers all helped one another even if they weren't asked to do so. I was a process worker for nearly 40 years.

I became a temporary supervisor for a while at Levers and I really liked that, it was the best job I had at Levers, I was disappointed at the outcome of it. I had become a chargehand, in those days a leading hand, the supervisor then was off from work, so I was allowed to take over. I put all my soul into it. I even think that the other workers respected me in a way. I always tried to be fair. I would put up the shift list, and I would have the other men coming up to me and if they disagreed with it I would try and alter the list to suit all.

It wasn't the fact that I was a Corporal in the T.A., I never took the line of " you do as I say " if you know what I mean. I was in charge of men and I tried listen to what they had to say. I'd say OK you do it your way and we'll see how we get on . And if it didn't work they would go out and do it my way, not only would I tell them what to do I had to listen to their points of views as well. The manager then did not have a lot of respect from the workers as he was disliked by them. He wasn't a bad bloke, I remember, he was fair and he would stick up for you. But the workers couldn't stand him.

One foreman was transferred to Nigeria , Africa , so a vacancy came up and the manager Jack Jones , came to me and told me he had put my name down for the job, he said on the side it was my job, before I even went up in front of the board. Just before it all happened the manager had retired, everyone said it would be me who got the job.

The only thing you could get out of a manager there was your Christmas dinner , which you had to pay for. He came in and changed who was to get the job, so I was disappointed.

I found out later that the chap who got the job had been inviting the new manager round to his house for meals.

Jack Jones has passed away now. He was the best boss I ever had at Levers.
This new manager asked me to show the new man the ropes, the one who'd beaten me to the job. I wasn't too pleased I can tell you.

Jack Jones said " Oh no, he's my leading hand and he's on my shift , you've shit on him enough." At that time I was thinking about packing it in. He was a good man was Jack Jones , he was known to be a bit rough at times , but he was fair and a good boss on the whole.

They weren't all good though , there were some not so good ones too. There was one boss, however, that worked down in the mills, the animal feeds place. The gang I was in were out on loan. I was the chargehand for some of the lads when they were transferred to the farm from the flour mill. The foreman there , he was unfair to the lads and was treating them badly, so I told him , look, we were transferred down here, I was the one in charge of these lads. He said I'm the supervisor down here and you have got no authority over these men . So this led to words, I didn't agree so I said well OK let's have the personnel down and sort it out as my men were very unhappy.

So personnel came down and agreed with me. I was quite surprised, but they were looking at it from their point of view, you see, ... they wanted harmony , people working together, not problems. So I looked after the gang. Quite right too. We did a good job, had no more hassle , and were back in our own place by the next day.

There were some jobs that were worse than others , times varied there, you got the burst pipes, cleaning them up was hard work, but I was a young man then , so I could cope with just about anything that was thrown at me. We'd have a go at anything.

Safety was very tight then though . One manager , Jack Lee was very strict on safety, the reason was that he had lost four fingers in a machine, there was no guard on the machine. Jack was a Junior Manager at the time. From then on every machine had a guard on it. He was the instigator of that , Jack was.

There were very few accidents. One time, whilst I was on nights, the managers then worked 24 hours, you never knew when they were coming. We used to do a lot of the cleaning of a night time. You can imagine what the floor would be like. Covered in soap, soapowder and such.

They had a special cleaning gang, that's all they did, just the cleaning. A few of them got fed up of these managers coming in and not knowing when they were coming in. So they decided to leave some of the scum on the floor. The managers came in that night and the next thing you know there were three of them straight on their backsides.

Next thing it was, Jack Lee again, new signs were placed onto notice boards "DANGER .... SLIPPERY FLOOR, CLEANING IN PROGRESS" . But he never took it out on anyone, he said it was management's fault , we should let you men know when we are coming in. From then on they never bothered us, and they informed us when they would come in .

Coming to the outbreak of war I was on two-to-ten. There were loads of lads in the T.A. there , and they were coming up and saying , that's it , we're off. I was the last to go, I thought they had forgotten me. Then George Tasker came up to me and said , well , you might as well go now too , there's nothing for you to do here.

I got home and I didn't know about reporting. We had to report to the drill hall in Grange Road West. I was in the house and my mum asked why I was home so early. I said we'd been sent home as the plant had closed down , everybody was sent home.

Then my Father came in, and said to me "Where the hell have you been? You're posted as a deserter , you were supposed to be at the drill hall for 10 o'clock. "

So we had to get there double quick . Thankfully the C.O., who worked at Levers remember , said that there had been a breakdown in communications somewhere. I was in there and then, for five years. That was September 3rd and just after Christmas I was captured at Dunkirk and went to Colditz .The conception was that it was an officers camp. But there were other ranks too, orderlies and the like, people who looked after the officers , just as they would had they not been captured. We were treated as other ranks by the officers.We left Colditz, and to this day I have no inclination to go on the continent for my holidays, as back then we walked around most of it. We walked through Holland, Belgium and all over the place before we got to our camp.

After the war I had some leave coming before I went back to Levers . Of course, when I was a Prisoner of War the company paid my mother half of my wages. But they did slip up as while I was away they wrote to my mum saying that they didn't know how long the war would last , so therefore they were going to cross us off their books. But it was the law that all servicemen's jobs would be safe , so Levers had to rescind that letter you see.

Levers was really the only thing available anyway. I did talk about leaving it a few times, I was tempted to leave . A friend of mine's brother-in-law who was a foreman at Octel, he said to me , why don't you come here? So I came home and said I was going to go to Octel. "Oh! no you're not says my mum, you can stay where you are". So I could have packed up and gone to Octel but I decided to stay there.

The conditions then were pretty good. You got your free overalls, later on you got your free safety boots, safety glasses. We were quite well looked after. Looking back, you have to say that the first Lord

Leverhulme was an exceptional man.

Even so , we lost a lot of people when Vauxhalls opened , they all went there because the money was good. But after a while they would come back , they said it they were fed up , "it's no bloody fun walking from Ellesmere Port to Birkenhead at three o'clock in the morning.

As far as strikes and that goes , one lad who was an old timer there when I was there told me that one time years ago ,the office staff went on strike and the process workers came out and backed them up in sympathy. Then another time the process workers went on strike , but the office staff never came out. The workforce were always very wary of backing anybody after that. That's what I was told anyway.

I think I would do it again, to have gone to Levers, but I always had this feeling I wanted to go in the army. I'd have still been a young man walking out of the army.

I wouldn't go there today if I was 18. No I wouldn't go back . I hear so much about the dissatisfaction of the staff . I've never known people who work there to say ... Oh I wish to God I was like you .... finished ... out of it . I went when I was 64, the company asked me to go, I had forty years and didn't pay any pension , Levers did all that for me.

But today I've never known anything like it. I have quite a lot of friends in Sunlight, and it seems to be the general thought that "if they come up with the right money, then I'll go." It's more or less, it reminds me now , more or less , of a Prisoner of War camp now. One time you could have a wander round the factory, now you can't, you have to have a pass card for everything. There's no canteen, it's all vending machines, you have to have a card even for the machine, people there today are very dissatisfied.

I have a very low opinion of the company these days , it's only in recent years they've started to give a sort of tea party for pensioners, it's a sort of charitable thing and I hate bloody charity. They had it at Hulme Hall there , and the entertainment that they used to shove on, ... well ....all I can say is that is was like Fred Carnos... they were cheap acts!

They don't treat the pensioners that well today. People only recently started having to pay into the pension funds. Levers had that much money in the funds that they didn't need to get people to pay in. So if they had that much then why didn't they give the pensioners a bit more money ? There's more than me need it , some a lot older than me, in their 90s , ex- Lever men who did hard jobs for them.

But I've no regrets about working there, it was a good job, we were well treated, we had a health centre, dentist, you name it, you had it. Now we get a newsletter now and again. It used to be a magazine, named The Port Sunlight News, now it's called the Lever Mirror. It's full of stuff about what the company are doing and all that , but to us people , who are retired it means nothing, just obituaries , which are sad to see , sometimes you know them , old friends .

Bloody hell I wasn't there for 43 years was I ?

With Greetings and Every Good Wish

For myself and colleagues I wish to present you with this record of your response to your Country's call for recruits, preservists. We are all prouder of you than our feeble words can express. You are part of that brave army of Britons and Allies who are today the Saviours of Empire and the preservers of Peoples, Justice and Civilisation throughout the World.

Neither in Greek nor in Roman History are there to be found records that surpass your heroic devotion to your Country and your King. May you have a speedy return bearing with you the laurels of Victory won and Peace restored— Yours Sincerely

W H Lever

On the Previous page is a copy of a hand written letter from 'Billy ' Lever to those employees who had been 'called' to the 'Great War ', 1914 - 1918. It reads :

With greetings and every good wish

For myself and my collegues I wish to present you with this record of your response to your Country's call for recruits and reservists - we are all prouder of you than our feeble words can express. You are part of that brave army of Britons and Allies who are today the saviours of Empire and the preservers of Peoples, Justice and Civilisation throughout the world.

Neither in Greek nor in Roman History are there to be found records that surpass your heroic devotion to your Country andyour King . May you have a speedy return bearing with you the laurels of victory won and peace restored.

Yours Sincerely

W.H.Lever.

The unveiling of the war memorial in the center of the village circa 1928 ?

Stan Williams
D.O.B 17.4.30

Process Worker
Worked in Levers
1950-1990

First of all you had to apply for a job. Part of the drill was once you were interviewed by the Employment Officer, if you were taken on you were then taken down to the Department you were going to work in and sort of introduced to the Supervisor. Following that you started the next day be it on days, or on shift work.

My first day as I remember, when I went down into the room where I was working which was No. 1 Frame Room, I was introduced to the Supervisor down there, a chap named Jack Rowe, who was a small, rotund gentleman. He took me down to the gang who I was going to work with. That gang was called the Loading Out gang. The job consisted of two men and a boy who were responsible for loading out slabs of soap which had been cut by the cutters.

I was introduced to the guy I was going to work with, Charlie Sproston. Charlie Sproston and I have remained firm friends from that first day right up to the present day. We were responsible for loading soap out of rows. There was a row of soap with 22 frames in each row. It was the loaders responsibility once those frames of soap had been stripped and cut by the mechanical cutters, we then manually loaded them out onto trucks and together with the help of a young lad we run them out the rows. Then the young boy was responsible to run them out onto what they termed the patches, which were the areas of work where the soap was barred, that is cut into slabs and then people on the other side of the cutters put them out onto racks. They were called pilers and basically that was my first day in Levers.

Basically the job was just shown to you because at that time it was basically just manual work, there was only a modicum of skill attached to the job. It was basically a labouring job. That was basically my job, that's the job I started on and the job I sort of stayed on, although during my time in that room, if and when it was necessary you were taken and shown other jobs, and given a little bit of training. So it was a case that you had a job but if there was somebody sick or you were wanted somewhere else you'd be utilised anywhere within that area of work.

As a matter of fact, I'd just come out of the Army. It was my first job when I got demobbed. Prior to going in the Army I'd had a lot of jobs as a young lad and when I went in the Army I took up a trade as a burner/welder and fully intended to take up that job when I came out of the Army. I had a trade certificate from the Army but found it was very difficult to be accepted into the unions so I was a bit disappointed. Other jobs that I'd tried, and I'd tried many, just didn't satisfy me. So a guy who was demobbed with me, a local lad, just said "look, they're taking guys on at Levers, shall we go up, it'll put us over". So I went to Levers at that particular time. I never intended to stay for 40 years at Levers, it was my first time working in a factory too, and it was just an off chance we took. We both went up to Levers, both started at the same time, and taken on in the same Department.

To be perfectly honest, I'd never really heard that much about Lever Bros., apart from two people I knew who had spent a certain amount of time at Lever Bros. and they'd given the Company a good report. It had a good reputation for looking after its employees. It was considered a job for life if you kept your nose clean. It wasn't with that intention I went there , it was just that we were looking for work. It seemed to be a good idea at the time. We were lucky enough to be taken on and the first job I was offered I did quite readily in the hope that maybe something better might come along. I found it very hard to settle down there at first because it was my first time in a factory and it seemed that everywhere you looked there was a clock and time seemed to drag. Anyway that was my job and the ensuing weeks and months after that was in the loading of soap.

Where I worked in that particular room one side of the room was male dominated; that was the frame room and the packing floor or the cutting floor and the other side, separated by about 20 yards was the packing area and that was basically female dominated. We didn't intermingle in those days. There were jobs in Port Sunlight where later on in years women and men worked alongside each other ,and do now, but not then so much.

It was run by a team of management which consisted of two managers, one had overall responsibility, that was Jack Lee, and if you ask me to give an honest impression of Jack Lee, he was one of the most ignorant men I've met in my life. His assistant was a guy named Charlie Atkinson. Charlie was a rough and ready type of man, he'd 'f' and blind at everybody in sight, women as well but he was a fair-minded sort of a fellow. Then the rest of the management crew was made up of supervisors. The first guy I was introduced to was a fella named Jack Rowe. He wasn't a bad sort but I don't think I would trust him as far as I could throw him. There was another guy named Jack Roberts who was a straight guy from the shoulder. He expected you to graft and once you'd done your graft you were alright.

After the Frame Room a new development of frame soap was coming in to being in the middle 50's and I was then transferred to a place they called the Experimental Process Unit which was a new innovation in making soap. Instead of being framed it was being milled and chilled, instead of soap being left to mature for 5-7 days before you could work on it , this was a continual process of liquid soap coming into the mill being chilled and pushed through a plodder at high speed, aerated and it came out in an continuous slab of soap which was then cut, put out to cool and then barred and boxed within the process of an eight hour shift. I worked there on days for about three to six months and then that particular job went into a shift work situation and I stayed in that work place on shift work for two or three years. I found that shift work didn't agree with me, as a matter of fact I developed an ulcer as a result of working on shifts, and the medical opinion at the time was to get me off shifts.

I approached the management who weren't too happy about putting me into a day work situation because I was a trained operative in a relatively new situation. However, I was then put back into the Frame Room, on days, and then work tailed off because of the new system and they didn't require the same number of men in the frame room. So I was then transferred into various other jobs. I did a year in Engineering as an engineering mate and from there I spent 18 months in the Seed Crushing mills and Animal Foods which was an experience I'd rather forget because it was one hell of a job. You were spitting animal food out all over the place.

The conditions were atrocious in there, in the Compound Mill. It was basically dust, wherever you went you were swallowing it. It was on your sandwiches, in your clothes, your hair. The areas where you were supposed to eat, the mess rooms and canteens were always in a filthy state. There were rats all over the place 24 hours a day. It was a horrific place to work.

It was part of BOCM and Lever Bros. It was called Lever BOCM Foods then. It was a dirty, horrible, stinking place to work. There were two gangs I operated in there. One was on the Intake gang which was responsible for taking in all the raw materials, stowing them in warehouses until they were required in the production . I was in the warehouse for a short time trucking out, loading vehicles in that area, but that was one hell of a stinking job. I was determined to either get out of there or pack up.

From the Compound Mill I got a job in Raw Materials and that's where I spent the rest of my time, 30 odd years, which was a job I basically liked because virtually it was a job where you were your own boss. You were responsible for the intake of a whole host of chemicals from caustic soda, hydrocarbons, oils, you name it we handled it. You knew what you had to do and what you were responsible for and so you saw the boss maybe twice a day.

There were some rotten jobs too when I worked on raw materials. Cleaning tanks out, caustic soda with no protective clothing in those days, a pair of wellingtons, a pair of rubber gloves and a pair of goggles were all you got. As a consequence I've got a nasty caustic burn. Down on the dock too where you had 1000 ton tanks, cleaning whale oil tanks out, they were stinking jobs them.

But then you'd be expected to turn your hand to anything. When you were employed at Levers on the process you were employed by Levers and you were expected to go where they wanted you to go. So if you were on the slabbing and they said we want you down the dock, you'd go down on the dock. They'd take you down there, they might walk you down or it might be in a company van , show you where you reported to and the rest was left to you. And then that's your place of work until you're told otherwise. So if you could walk to work from home before and then you had to start paying bus fares to wherever you where next , you're out of pocket. Nor was there always an increase in job rate. They paid a basic wage when I first started , followed by a job rate and that job rate started at something about six to eight shillings , and it went up to about 30 shillings in those days.

My first pay packet was roughly about £4.00 for 42 hours work.

That was a full, mans wage, take home pay. In comparison with other jobs of a similar nature it was always thought that Levers paid that little bit over the odds than other companies in the area. I don't think many people would argue with that, until Vauxhall's came on the scene, then things changed.

I enjoyed the work I did in Raw materials because it gave you a variety of jobs to do, you weren't stuck in one place. We had various work places around the factory. Part of my job was being responsible for pumping various chemicals to various departments and it gave you a lot of freedom, freedom which I enjoyed because I hated working inside. It was worth a fiver a week to me because I enjoyed doing what I was doing. I was out, you were out in all kinds of weather, but you got used to that. I really did enjoy that part of my job.

I didn't become a steward for USDAW until the 1960's. Simply and solely, I was always a member of the union, but the union was not strong in those days, because people weren't really interested in trade unions. There's never a job I'd do for nothing, certainly not for Levers. As Shop Steward, I thoroughly enjoyed doing that but that was by the way.

I've always been interested in union activities and I've always been a member of a trade union. When I first joined the trade union in Port Sunlight in the early 50's the trade was governed by what they then termed the Soap, Candle and Edible Fats. That was the negotiating body, it was like a wage council. They were responsible for the conditions in that industry, not just Lever Bros. but all similar industries. The union wasn't strong in those days. I put myself up for election. First and foremost I've got to say I've always been a member of the union but I've always been a bit of a rebel. A rebel in as much that, I suppose due to impatience I used to think things could be changed overnight and it's only as you grow older, with more experience you realise that's not the case.

When I went to the Branch meetings I wasn't a very popular person in those days because I used to say to the Branch officers a whole host of things that I would never dream of saying now because I felt they were not doing their best for all the membership. It was only through inexperience. I thought things should change and it didn't happen that way. I became Shop Steward in 1967 and I represented Raw Materials right up to the time I retired.

When I first became Shop Steward I'd followed union activities for most of my working life but I didn't know an awful lot about trade unions at that time. I was given a very good piece of advice from the Branch Secretary at the time, who became a very great friend of mine, Tony Maclean, who said to me "Keep your mouth shut until you learn enough to open it".

That was one of the best pieces of advice that was ever given to me relative to trade union activities. He became my Branch Secretary and I became, after a few years, in 1975/6 the Branch Chairman and stayed Branch Chairman until unfortunately ill health in the last two to three years of my employment forced me to give it up.

I don't think Levers thought a lot of me then. I was a bit of a firebrand and used to shout the odds to them. There was a lot of finger wagging and hot under the collar stuff across the table but I can honestly say that in all of those years it didn't matter how many cross words I had with management, I could always meet them the next day on a civilised footing. There would be no animosity.

I'm not saying that was always the case. I found that was with more top level management. With middle line management there was a lot of people I had contact with on behalf of the membership who bore personal grudges. One or two of those people, even if they were wrong wouldn't admit they were wrong. I've met some nasty members of management and supervision in 40 years at Port Sunlight. I've come into contact with a lot of real characters and I've met some really nice gentlemanly people in management too. One of the best bosses was a guy named Ray Frobisher who was only a young fella but he was very fair minded, but he was of the newer school. On the whole I always found that if you were sure of your case, knew you were right, stuck to your guns and were able to prove you were right, management in general would recognise that fact and more than meet you halfway.

The worst dispute we were involved in was in the late 60's early 70's. We were tied up in Levers with enzymes coming on site - they were supposed to be a new innovation to make your wash that much whiter. I think everybody including management and indeed the research chemists at that time were completely ignorant about enzymes. Enzymes used to come on site in kegs and they were then entered into the process. They were handled by hand. There was all sorts of spillages, those spillages were basically brushed up. It was found that enzymes could and did become injurious to the chest, could cause chest problems. If you were susceptible to chest problems then obviously it wasn't in your best interests to work with enzymes.

We negotiated with the Company because of the people's feelings about working with these enzymes. A payment which was called an enzyme payment, was paid to personnel who worked in the areas where enzymes were used so there was a perimeter drawn around the factory. Like everything else that payment at that time was only paid to Production Workers, plus tradespeople, like fitters and electricians, who were working in the area. We also introduced, after long arguments with the Company, that tradespeople and other people could go in there on an eight hour basis and would still be open to the enzymes and should, therefore, also be included in the payment.

We as a Branch took time to make some enquiries into enzymes and how injurious they were to people's health and Dr Murrey, who was the TUC's Doctor, wrote a thesis on it and it was his opinion that enzymes were injurious to health and could cause asthma, chronic bronchitis and a whole host of other complaints. However, we wanted to get shut of enzymes as a union, because we felt that no amount of payment would suffice for good health. However, the guys who worked in that area suddenly decided they didn't mind working in enzymes for a price. They said the price they wanted to work for was something like £10.00 per week over and above the basic rate , and the Company wouldn't hear of it. The workforce in that area, the NSD Department, that stood for Non Soap Detergents, took it into their heads to walk off the job, unofficially.

They went to unofficial dispute, against our wishes that they should carry on working with a view to us negotiating. We knew the Company wouldn't negotiate under duress so we were at a stalemate. I spent more time on site then than any other time, 48 hours I was away from home, stuck on site, negotiating with top level management. By this time it wasn't just factory management that were involved, it was management from Head Office at Kingston.

We were dealing directly with the Chairman and Personnel Director. We reached an impasse. During this time we knew, as Branch Officials, there was no way the Company would negotiate in any form unless we got the workforce back to work. After a lot of discussion with the workforce we asked them to come back to work so that we could negotiate on their behalf as there was nothing we could do for them while they were out on unofficial stoppage.

By this time five days had gone by. They had unofficial pickets on the gate who were interfering with the wagons, getting them to turn back, not come in with loads, loads which were not for their own department but which were for other departments and our concern was that if they were stopping lorries coming in with stuff for other areas of work then those other areas of work would be laid off too. After five days we were able to get them back to work on their own terms which did not include any increase because by this time they were feeling the pinch, they knew they wouldn't get any money. They'd been working large slices of overtime so they were feeling the pinch , so they came back to work. Shortly after that the Company withdrew enzymes from the market altogether, of their own volition. I think it was because they knew they couldn't go on putting enzymes into their products without paying a more realistic figure to the workers. It was becoming too expensive. That was my worst time as a steward.

There have been some daft disputes too over the years, but they've not included large numbers of people. They've only been in departments, in shifts, inter-shift disputes and that sort of thing, were the guy's thought somebody's getting more overtime than him that sort of thing. There were many silly disputes of that nature.

To be honest and to be fair, when I first started at Port Sunlight, they tried to be safety conscious but I don't think they were very successful at it then. They've always had health facilities and surgeries and if you cut yourself or got a splinter in your finger there was never any hassle about allowing you to go up to the surgery for treatment. Accidents and bad accidents were few and far between. I've seen one or two guys go into the dock and had to have their stomachs pumped out when they've been dragged out.

Unfortunately, I've seen one or two of my old workmates who were involved in bad accidents. That was two guys who were on the sulphination plant, which is part and parcel of where I worked later on, who were burnt very badly with sulphuric acid. Burnt to the degree where they bore the scars all their lives , although the scars weren't so bad that they spoilt their appearance. I've also seen one guy who was blown off a tank with an explosion. They were probably the worst accidents I ever saw in Levers. There have been fatal accidents during my time in Port Sunlight though. One was relative to a guy who was crushed between the buffers of a train.

To Levers credit ,in my experience once a person has been injured then no expense has been spared in helping that person or their family in trying to give that person the best medical attention and making certain that the family is financially reasonably secure. Even when death has occurred.

As a Shop Steward there were always little bits of jealousies which arose, again basically in later life when the equality situation came out when women then started to enjoy the same rates of pay as the men. Women wanted that little bit more once they enjoyed the equality of payment then they saw no reason, and rightly so, why they shouldn't be included in overtime rotas and so forth. In those cases it did create a bit of division between the female and male workforce. In some cases the women had very good cases and we were able to secure their rights in that situation but in other situations it wasn't practical to expect women not only to work overtime but in certain jobs because they just couldn't do them - too physical or whatever.

In the early days there was always that division between the blue collar worker and the white collar worker shall we say. When I first started there that was prevalent. Jumped up time clerks thought they were members of high society, they used to look down their noses at the guys in overalls so to speak. That did go on and even in the main offices, once you got into the main offices, if you had an occasion to go into the main offices in the early days, white collar workers did, for some reason, think they were a step above.

Things did change, probably the trade union helped a lot in this direction. In the late 60's, 70's and onwards from there , people became a bit more liberated in their thoughts and they thought well, we're all here to get the best living we can and we've got a lot in common. I think they turned a corner and went hand in hand in lots of ways, particularly in relation to wage negotiations and looking for better conditions for work.

I must confess that when I first started there I thought to myself ..... If I do six months here that will be my lot ... , because I found it difficult to settle into the regime of factory life. Then time went by and probably I think what kept me there eventually was the fact that I got out of the inside environment and was working in an outside situation. I got interested in my union activities and I think I can honestly say that for 35 of those 40 years I enjoyed it.

Of course we had lots of characters in Levers too. They were all over. There were too many to remember and I can't really sort one out. Like everywhere else, there were comedians, there were guys who were absolute nutters. I can remember one, we're going back to the early days when the unions were more or less just catching on and management couldn't really grasp that their power was having to be shared. There was a guy, a college educated guy who,for some reason ended up at Port Sunlight, a lad named Martin. He was a bit of a hippie, it was early 70's, he had long hair, a beard and always wore sandals. We were having a lot of problems in the NSD Department and Martin was never out of the bosses office. The Manager, a fella named Stan Smith, a really rough and ready character, but he would never ask a man to do something he wouldn't do himself, didn't get on with Martin because Martin was always in his office wanting something for the lads.

On this particular day Martin bowled up to his office and knocked on the door, Smith's got his head down and says "Come in", Martin walks in, Stan Smith lifts his head up and says "Jesus Christ".
Martin said "No, Mr Smith, it's just Martin".
That just one instance of what some of them were like.

I've no regrets about staying so long there. If it's done one thing it's provided me with a lifetime of employment which I've been grateful for because when you look around in later years, I had security of employment. There were times when I could have packed up at Sunlight and gone to work for more money but those jobs weren't permanent positions. While it didn't pay lots of wages, conditions did improve through those 40 years. Eventually we were able to negotiate rates of pay in Lever Bros. Port Sunlight which were comparable with any company on Merseyside. So I would say that while I've had my ups and downs at Port Sunlight common sense prevailed and here we are. I think I would say that I would do it again.

But not today , I wouldn't like to do it these days. Of course things change. They never stay as they are. I've seen 40 years of change. Part of that change at the latter end of my working days I felt, maybe it was out of loyalty to the people I represented, I felt they were having the dirt done on them by a new breed of management. A management of hatchetmen. It might not have been their personal view but they, to protect their jobs, were given orders from the Heads of Unilever who after all were the Bankers of Lever Bros. Port Sunlight and they were given jobs to annihilate the workforce and I think that the way they've gone about reducing the workforce in Port Sunlight may be considered by some to be fair but I think they could have been fairer.

I think that what's left at Port Sunlight, like everywhere else, things change and the way the labour market is that maybe we're back to the 30's a bit at Port Sunlight whereby management are ruling by decree as opposed to through discussion and agreement. I've still got a lot of friends there and the guy who took over my job in the union still phones me up now and again. Some of the things he's told me it appears now because of the situation there even the unions have their hands tied. Where you always had an avenue for discussion with management at whatever level, now any decisions are a sort of fait accompli. Management call you in, advise you what they're going to do and leave it with you to relay back to the membership.

Obviously the underlying message is if you don't want to do it there's plenty of people who do. I think that's a shame. Through the years there was a good rapport built up between the workforce and management, generally speaking. It's a shame the way things are developing up there. I do think, speaking to people who still work there, they feel that management are not being as open with them as they used to be.

I always said I'd never live here in the village, by virtue of the fact that they were tied cottages, the houses went with the job. Two things changed me, a change of circumstance was one. We moved here in 1975, then the Housing Act changed whereby tied cottages were no longer part and parcel of your employment. In other words if you were sacked by Levers they couldn't chuck you out of your home. Prior to that they could. The reason we came to live here was we had our own house downtown which came under a clearance order. We were re-housed by the Council, the house we were given was a lovely house but unfortunately a lot of the people they put alongside us weren't, so as a result of that I applied for a house up here.

I'm a pensioner now and I suppose, to be fair, Levers treat you better than some companies. But they could treat them better. After all when you retired at Levers, going back a little while when things were more normal, you retired at 65 after whatever service. Your pension was relative to the number of years you'd put in. That was fair enough. Now you're retired at 60, I'm very happy about that. Whether I'd be happy if I'd only had 19 years of service in is a different matter because we're back to pensionable pay. In my own case I was a bit disappointed in the terms which were offered me when I retired. I put 40 years in there and for what I got from a pension point of view..... then I'm not arguing too much about that, but the lump sum they now get when they retire, well, I was a little bit put out.

I put 40 years in, there are people who are now retiring, one or two years after me with say 20 years service who are getting almost double the amount on their lump sum as I did. I think if Levers have gone wrong it maybe, and I'm trying to be fair, I think they maybe haven't given sufficient thought to pensioners pay off pay. My pension I'm quite happy with. Lever Bros. don't have any annual functions for pensioners. It has been proposed apparently on more than one occasion and the reason they give is that there are far too many pensioners for them to have a formal or even an informal get together.

To see the place now, flogging off the village properties. I think old Billy Lever would spin in his grave. I try to have an open mind on it because if you look around you Lever Bros. is going in a different direction. It's lost its paternal instincts and that's been long gone. The Estate has changed beyond recognition, relative to the well-being of the village.

There used to be the Estate Yard where they had all their own tradespeople, joiners, roofers and such like. That no longer exists. If you want a repair doing now a contractor comes and does the job. If you look at the gardens situation that's now been flogged off. Unilever is no longer responsible for the Parks and Gardens as such so the selling off of the village doesn't bother me. I believe in the freedom of people if they get the opportunity to purchase a house in Port Sunlight, good luck to them. I think some of the prices they're asking are ridiculous. How can you be expected to pay between £50,000 and £100,000 for houses which are over 90 years old ? The main reason they're paying those prices is because it's a listed village.

What maybe does bother me is where we go in the future. Whether it's a good thing long term I don't know. Port Sunlight is a village, it was known throughout the world as a village built by Billy Lever for his employees and maintained by Levers. That's no longer the case.

Stan Williams (3rd from right) meeting Queen Elizabeth II
during the companys' centenary celebrations in 1988.

Seen here at a company function, it looks like the inside of Hulme Hall, Stan Williams is the third from the left.

Betty Graham
D.O.B Over 21

Machine Operator
Worked in Levers
1946-1986

I worked in the flakes mainly. I went in the flakes department and we bagged all flakes up, soap flakes. I was a machine operator,

I can remember some of my first day. I know they gave me an overall right down to my ankles and one of them funny hats they used to wear then. Y'know them hats that you put all your hair in, and then somebody showed me the work , it wasn't the bosses, they used to leave the girls to show you what to do, y'know, and then we were bagging off, y'know, putting wires round the bags and bagging them off and then you had to push it on, it went onto a truck and then it went into the warehouse.

It was a sort of chute, a big cylinder, 'cause there was no machines going because they had no fitters - I suppose they had an odd fitter, y'know what I mean - but they never had, well they had a couple of fitters, but never . . . 'cause they were all away weren't they? And then we used to have to fill all these big Hitita bags . . .and then you wired then up, filled them up with 28lb in the sack, and don't forget I was only 14 and then I had to wire them up ,we had to move up and take turns, and we'd wire them all off and stack them on the truck.

The women had to do the lifting. And then, when we'd done that, we had to push it to the man. There was a man that took them into the warehouse. I didn't go on that; there was another, older lot of girls and they done big flake boxes for the ships, y'know, the wooden boxes, and they used to have nails hammered, going along, and the boxes would come along and they'd put them all on and away they'd go. And they had to lift the boxes, there was no men, you see.

We only got a 20 minute dinner hour - that's Irish isn't it? We only got 20 minutes for our dinner break . We started at twenty to eight until half five; we were on I think a 44-hour week then. Then it went to 42, then it went to 40 and 37, y'know, dropped down. And then after that, after you done this Hitita thing, it was really, really dusty . . .

They were Lux flakes, But the hitita wasn't; they were very strong for on the ships, for doing the decks or whatever they done with them, I don't really know, laundry maybe. I don't know, when you're young you don't take any notice. And what did we do then. After the day, you had to scrub right along on your hands and knees, scrub the floor on your hands and knees, not mopping, scrubbing. Used to put parafin (weren't supposed to) in the water to stop the soap, 'cause you couldn't get the soap up you see, couldn't stop the soap from foaming up. And then it got busy, the flakes were coming back on the market, the packets - you know the blue packets. They come on the market and so they put 7 a shift. Well at 16 I was on relay, six to half-two.

A relay is a shift, you see. At 16 I was on relay and I lived downtown then and I had to run along the dock road there to get the bus. The bus used to come at 10 to 5, to get us to Sunlight because it was a double-O and the double-O took us from Laird Street, by the docks. Park Entrance, pick us up, go right along to Sunlight, go along the depot and go all the way to the Planters, as they called it, it was called the Planters as it wasn't called Stork, it was called the Planters.

Where Stork is now, it was called Planters, I don't know why. And then we'd come back. It was the same coming home. We used to finish at half-two; I'd get in at three. And this is where all the trouble is I think now with the kids. We were so tired we didn't have time to go out and do any vandalising. I was so tired at 16 when I finished. If you look at them at 16 now, y'know.

I didn't even have a clue then about working life. Only that me mum used to think it was a good job and everybody went to Sunlight. If you can get in Sunlight it was O.K. she said. There were five of us girls there, all of us, and my sister was there and she was in No. 4 with all the girls with the shampoos, she used to do shampoos called Eve. They were like the little Cephos powders.And there were about 200 kids on that, about 14 years of age.

I didn't know whether I liked it or I didn't like it. D'you know what I mean? I used to say "I'm not staying there" and they'd say "You will stay, you'll stay, I'm telling you you'll stay", 'cause I had no father, you see. My dad died when we were all young, so of course, I thought it was terrible. But then I got to know the girls, and that, y'know. And of course, me being big they put me on all the things that the big girls were on, the girls of 18 or 19, so I was along with them, and then they put me on this relay. That was smashing, I used to love that. That was on packing all the boxes of flakes for the shops.

There were only so many done because they were just coming back on the market after the war and we packed them all and sent them off. That I enjoyed, we had some fun, like, 2 till 10 when they'd all go home. The only thing I didn't like was on a Friday, the factory used to finish at 10 past 4, so from 10 past 4 to 10 o'clock was a long time, but then after that . . . . I wasn't in the one place, I got dust . . . I nearly had a sinus, y'know, so I went to the printing department. That was alright. From the printing department I went on the quality, going round collecting the stuff off the machines, samples for the bosses and all that. You had to make sure everything was perfect - everything that come off the line was perfect. This could be anything, Persil, Surf, all the toilet soaps, Comfort, Dual, the hard soaps, Lifebuoy and Sunlight and all that.

It was a good firm to work for then. I mean they always looked after you. What annoyed me, when you got paid sick pay, you see, if you were off, and I was never ever off, and I couldn't wait to be sick, to be 21. As soon as I arrived at 21 they brought the age down to 18.

It's true, soon as I was 21 they brought the age down to 18. Honest to God, about a week before, and of course you got 12 weeks' sick pay if you were off, but me mum wouldn't let us be off. She wouldn't let us be off, honest to God she wouldn't. She'd say "You're not staying off here, beat it" and she'd make us go to work. So much so , when I was young, It was really bad but I thought, I can't go home, Mum will think that I'm skiving like, so I went to my sister's. She worked there with us. I said "The health centre said I've got to go home" and she said "You'd better not", so I said "What will I do? They told me I've got to". So she said "Well here, go and sit in the Gaumont" and her and her mate gave me 1/3d each, half a crown, and I went and sat in the Gaumont until they come back. Gospel that.

You know, the Park Entrance, we lived round there, and I went and sat in the Gaumont. They sent me home from work and I didn't go home - I went and sat in the Gaumont - because mum didn't believe in you staying off on the sick. They said now give her your money on Thursday and I always handed me pay packet over to mum, always. Even until I was grown. So she said, "Just say you had to take your money out and we'll give you the half crown" because all I got was £1

2s 6d for the whole week and they used to take 4d or 5d for your stamp. It was 3d return bus fare on the bus from where we were - the old 3d. You had to hang on to that 'cause if you lost it you'd have to walk home 'cause you had no more money. They gave me the half crown to put in me wage packet. But that's how much they gave us.

I used to take my own butties in for the relay. Bacon was on ration and my mother used to save my coupons for the bacon to put on my butties for work. If not, that would be it.

This day, they'd had a clear out. They had no lockers or nothing like now, they're all modern aren't they? You used to have to put it in a box like that on the floor and Lizzie Clampet threw them out. That was the boss, she was the supervisor and she didn't know they were my butties and she flung them out and when I got in the canteen the girls said "She's flung your butties out, your bacon butties".

Well, there was murder. We had the personnel down and all I was saying was "That was me mam's 6oz of bacon that you've threw away". Anyway, they had to give me a free meal, 'cause I had no money', because we were really poor, y'know, and they'd thrown this sodden bacon away. But that's all there was, a canteen, and there was like . . . you had to go down and sit there and eat your meal and you only got 20 minutes' break.

Well you get an hour now but I think it's gone back to half an hour now and you used to only get 20 minutes like 'cause it was a working 20 minutes, what they'd call a working 20 minutes. You got paid for it, kind of thing, and it was only 20 minutes. It wasn't half an hour and dawdle back - right on the job, know what I mean?

It was a long day. We worked very hard but it was better. Like, when they ended up the way they were they were getting away with murder and yet you didn't have the same atmosphere as you did when you were younger or on the lines. There was more atmosphere with girls, y'know, more clannish.

There weren't many men around in the factory then. The men did come into it on the end, but mostly girls, gangs of girls. The men done the heavy things but then there come as you know sex equality. They were half and half you know on the machines and off the machines. We worked like slaves, we really did. We really worked like slaves. You'd go home knackered, really.

My favourite job was when I went over in the printing because I was bad with this dust complaint and they put me on doing the tea, y'know you met everybody, and I had to give me job up and I couldn't afford it so they said, well we'll find you a job, would you go on the tea.

They used to make tea on the trolley for the girls and the men and it was free. So that's what I did and honestly it was smashing, really really smashing, 'cause you met everybody, good fun. Even the fellows that brought the wagons come to you. You met more people like that and I'm that type of person, yap to them, y'know what I mean?
I didn't do it for that long , but I did do it in the printing 'cause then I went over to the quality, you see. But that was the best job. There was more to it. You met everybody and you seen everybody and it was a job you'd go on your own, because that was left to you and you did it the best way you could. Whereas if you're with a gang, well you'd need the others to be just as responsible as you, but when you've got a job to do on your own you do it to the best. It was great.

Because my chest was really bad, y'know. But Levers were to blame because you used to have what you call blow-outs with the dust and flakes and they'd blow right out and we couldn't see. They had to close the department down. Don't know whether the Health came in, I don't know. But they had to close it down and people got moved around and I was off sick then. First I had to go to the Ear, Nose and Throat place in Liverpool. Yeah,and I finally got paid sick! Anyway, I went to the Ear, Nose and had tests and they said it was this dust, you see so then they couldn't leave me in the room. They had to move me and I went over there.

Well, yeah, a case of having to it really was, but it was one of the best moves, really. It's really good when you get on to something like that. It wasn't soft but it was good. 'Cause there was about 400 people then in the printing and you were doing for 400 people . . .

The worst job I had there was .....Oh, the Pears. But I enjoyed most of it but sometimes . . . the job was alright, I didn't dislike that, didn't dislike the Pears at all and I didn't dislike the people, they were all smashing, but the place itself was absolutely terrible .

The Pears place was putrid and the heat was something else. Honest to God, the heat and the smell and everything about it was the worst. Really, we should've got double pay for being there, but the job . . . and that was one of the heaviest in my lifetime . . .

Well there again it was packing, but the girls had to lift all big trays of soap. I didn't do it because we were in this different section but the girls had to lift great big trays of soap, wooden. Honest to God I don't know how they done it. Quite honestly, they were more like men and they had to lift it, young girls and that. I don't know how anybody done it.

It smelled bad too, like ether. They had . . . alcohol it was, it's all done by alcohol you see so it was absolutely the worst. But it wasn't the worst as work goes. You understand what I'm trying to say? The place itself was terrible but the work didn't bother me. None of the work ever bothered me. It was so hot because they had to have the temperature for this soap. It had to be like hand-made, if you understand what I mean, so it was absolutely disgusting. The conditions and the heat, it was no good. That was the worst really. It was worst for most people yet if they got moved they'd say "I'm not going out". You got moved around sometimes and they'd say "I'm not going to another department" 'cause they liked the girls, the people.

The girls were great, smashing. They've all been good that I've worked with, really. I couldn't really say that any of the girls were no good. . . If you get in a gang, it was smashing, you couldn't say oh, it's terrible there. Girls like their own department they start off with. If they started off in Pears they love it. If they started off in the flakes, it's the same in the flakes. If they started off in the printing - you see it's what you're used to, all round. But now you see, that's all gone. They've all been closed down. The Pears have been pulled down. They make it in India now.

I wouldn't dare pinch anything for home. She warned us, you pinch anything and you'll take it every foot of the way back. She always said that to us, me mum. You will take it every foot of the way back, and me behind you, you ever come home here. That's the gospel that and people would say to her, like, when soap was short "You're alright, you've got five girls there". She used to buy shaving soap, they sold shaving sticks, you had to pleat them all round.

They were pleated, like a paper covering, yeah, cellophane. Our Joan, we used to call her the Queen of Bonus. She could do it so well, you had to do 12 pleats, well I never was on that, but she was. She used to do that and you got a bonus at the end of the week. Well we weren't on jobs that was bonus. But she was. She got the highest bonus every week. You had to pleat it all the way round, it was a tricky job. They used to pleat it then roll it, you had a little square like that, and you had to roll it, put your shaving stick in and roll it, and then pleat each end and all them pleats had to be within that little circle.

I went in dentifrice then ,they used to give dentifrice green, pink and like a blue I think it was and we had to pleat that. I tell you what, that was a nightmare. We were there till 11 o'clock at night.

There was a woman named Carrie Lee; she was the boss in there. She was a swine and she'd watch you, y'know. Girls loved it but you couldn't keep up with that. They were used to it and they had to pleat all them, like a little square block like that and a hole in the middle. It wasn't done by machine, it was all done by hand and yet they got the numbers out, y'know, when you think of it.

I had some good bosses and bad. Some of the better ones were , ... Miss Pearl in the printing and the manager, Jimmy Gerrard, he was nice. He'd worked his way up and he was a nice man, and fair.

When we were in No. Three, though Lizzie Clampet was a swine. She died, she lived up Kings Lane, that first house. But she was good to her own girls. She called them "my girls". Everybody hated her; maybe I shouldn't say hated her, but she was terrible. We used to have concerts in the canteen once a month, workers' playtime, y'know, and the first thing they'd say when they come on was they'd get the names off the girls and that so they'd make a joke about it and they all said about Lizzie Clampet, y'know.

But she was fair with you, although I didn't get on with her really, but she was fair to you and Jack Lee, the manager, he was great too. Perhaps other people mightn't have said but he was smashing with you, he was a good boss as managers go when you look what's there now.

Some were less good, but they never bothered me really. They might have bothered other people but they never bothered me because you see I think, if it's your worst boss, I could always stand up for myself, y'know what I mean, so it never bothered me. If you got told off you got told off and you must have done something to be told off. I wouldn't let them know that but I'd think it. No, I never thought any of them was really bad. . . but none of them was A1 'cause they were real Leverites, y'know, but . . . see when you got in a room like Levers they wouldn't like you if you worked in another room, but they looked after the girls that was their proper girls, their own.

No matter what you do they'd only treat you as their own and then perhaps you didn't like the boss. We were in the Pears and Jimmy Clare . . . now an awful lot didn't like him and other girls loved him.

He was smashing and he was really really fair. If you went to Jimmy Clare and said "She just did this to me", one of the bosses or that, and you went in the office and he'd say "Hang on, let's listen to this" and he was smashing. But all round the factory didn't like him 'cause they didn't know him but I did anyway and so did the other girls,

94

they loved him.

In the printing there were all what you call the "Leverites"; they walked down Greendale and they were home, weren't they? And they were in more or less tied houses and they couldn't do anything, they had to look after their jobs or they were out of the house. Well that's not there now you see so they don't do anything like that. Even if you wanted to do something wrong, stick by your guns regarding a job, they wouldn't join in with you because . . . I'm not saying they'd get the sack, like, but they wouldn't stick their neck out and in them days, if you were late twice a month you got the sack.

There was none of this union business. We did have a union in the printing but there was none of the union business. You knew the rules and if you were late, that's it, you were out. And we used to run . . . they used to have a whistle go at twenty to eight and you had to clock on by ten to eight. We'd have from about 500 yards to run in them days, get off the bus and run like hell and just about make it, because it you were late you'd had it.

I never became one, never ever was a Leverite. They were a nuisance actually. They were really a nuisance, you know, because they wouldn't do anything that they shouldn't. You know what I'm trying to say, like. They'd say "Oh no, I'm not doing that", although we never done anything we shouldn't have done . . . we'd never pinch or nothing like that but we'd bend the rules, more than a bit of lip, but they never done anything. If they said "Move that" and they shouldn't have done, well they'd have moved it, rather than say "Well I'm not doing it, let her do it". We used to always call them Leverites. But now all that's changed because most of them own the houses and them that's in them are only pensioners, so they don't have to worry about things like that. I suppose that's a good thing in one way.

I remember some accidents too, in the printing, they were painting but they were outsiders. The fellas fell from the roof right through the planks; we had about three in a week. I never seen anything that was major, that I can remember.

I was a union rep actually but in my time, there was a little union but it was always over pay things, there was never any real trouble . . there again, Leverites, they wouldn't join in, so we never had trouble. Well they did but they never done anything about it. Even if you wanted to, the Leverites wouldn't join in, so we never had any unrest. We did, but they wouldn't join in.

I shall always remember the girls though, Oh the girls, yeah. We used to have dances, departmental dances, every so often and it was smashing. You couldn't get a ticket. You had to get your ticket about six months before, y'know, one of them kind of dances. They were smashing. The next day they'd all start talking, who went off with so and so and all the married men and all the married women, well there were no married women because we didn't have them but you know what I mean.

They never had married women, they wouldn't let you come back. If you were getting married next week, you couldn't come back. In the last, say, 20 years they allowed them. They never had married women, only if you were a widow or something like that. Oh yes, you get them now, but they didn't then. My sister got married and she had a smashing job and she had to leave. You couldn't come back. In the 50s and 60s. But then it all changed, this new law come out. I think that was for the worse, really, 'cause once they come back and they didn't have the young ones there, and I think it's sad when the young ones could've had the jobs, 'cause there was no room for them then 'cause the others kept the jobs whereas before when they left, more young ones came in. I thought it was a bit sad then, for that.

There was nowhere else to go in those days so you just stayed at Levers. My sister Joan hated it in the Pears, she was glad to get out. Yet she wouldn't go anywhere else. She done forty years and she hated it. But it never bothered me.

Sometimes I used to think, "Well, I'll leave in a couple of years". I did think that sometimes but then the time and the years had gone by. When I'd heard about other girls going to other jobs, like Littlewoods, then those girls would say, don't leave, you don't get as much money and you don't get the sick money. I did get the sick money eventually but honest to God . . . I couldn't wait till I was 21, and the age come down to 18, honest to God.

They used to give you a week's holiday: here again, anybody who was 20, 'cause when you're 14 and they're 20 they were old, you know, I used to call them old maids, and I used to say "Can't have your holiday with the old maids". You only got a week and you had to be there a bit before you qualified for a week's holiday and my first week's holiday was in May and in that week was when King George got buried and I only got four days out of it. I nearly cried because everybody got a day off. First week's holiday the King died. He had to die when I was starting my holidays on the Monday. That's the truth that. My Aunty Kitty and me mam . . . . Me and this other girl we went in the office about it, me and Margaret Gilbert and said "The others have all put their holidays in and I've been here longer than you". I think it was that. The King died and we started our holiday, in May I think. In my mind it was May anyway.

I don't really have too many regrets about staying there so long, not really, no, I mean I had to work. If I'd had the money I'd have left, but then we didn't have the money, we were really poor, 'cause we were brought up with five kids and all our money had to go to me mum because she was a widow so really we couldn't leave and go somewhere else. But I think if I had me life over again I would go somewhere, keep moving somewhere, if I knew what I know now. I wouldn't do it over again. But then again, we were kept there forty years.

They always looked after you, you know what I mean? Used to give a free trip, you'd put your name down if you'd been there five years and you went to Holland. And we won that, both of us. We went for a week in Holland, they look after you. It was really great and they look after you something smashing. You go over there . . . there was only about twenty picked. They done it every other year. They picked twenty out of the factory to go over to Holland and there'd be twenty from Stork and there'd be twenty from Ireland and 20 from . . . all the companies belonging to Levers . . . make up about four or five coaches and they took you over to Holland. That week didn't come in with your holidays, that was another week.

We get our pension because we paid into it. I think they could do a little bit more for the pensioners. When I hear my mate who started work the same time as me with Littlewoods - they have outings for their pensioners and all that kind of thing. I really do think Levers should do more for us. You've got to be 80 before they give you a bouquet. Quite honestly I don't think they treat the pensioners as they should do but that's my opinion. They don't even seem to know us, even with forty years in . it doesn't mean a thing. For anybody with forty years, or twenty-five years plus, they could have done something, but they don't seem to. You get your pension fairly enough but that's the end of it. You see other firms doing things for pensioners.

They have their own pensioners' club but it's not run by Levers, it's run by themselves. The girls met up in the Levers club and they just done it themselves. Nothing's run by Levers, the company, and I think they could do, like Littlewoods - they put a train on and they take them for a meal and they take them somewhere else. But saying that, they always did look after you when you were there regarding sickness benefits and all them kind of things. But they did, you see, because some firms didn't give sick pay. Like Cammell Lairds , they didn't pay you when you were sick. No, that's what I mean.

When I got me watch, fifteen years you got a gold watch like, and my mum never had a watch, and she'd say "See the watch the girl got for fifteen years - I never got anything when I worked". I gave it to her. She bought me one for my 21st and when I got my fifteen years in . . . They stopped giving the watches when I was 21. You had to have the fifteen years after you were 21. People were kicking up terrible. They brought it back so I was back in for me fifteen years and I got the watch. Forty years I got a certificate for forty years and £800 to spend. Well they don't give you £800, you've got to spend the £800. You've got to go and spend it and give the invoice to them. They wouldn't give it to you for a holiday. Forty years, £800, not much is it?

I don't know much about what it's like these days, but from what I hear it's gone terrible, really down the nick. It's not like it used to be. Of course, nothing's like it used to be.

It's a shame really, when you look back at all the hundreds and hundreds of girls, and I mean hundreds. When I started there they used to have a man outside the gate and they had a contract with the Corporation and there'd be forty buses at least on the 51 route and they'd queue all down and the man would put you each on and send the buses out. Now they just have the ordinary bus service now, you know what I mean, and it's a shame really. It's gone, just like that.

I don't know. I think they could have done a little bit more, even when we left at forty years. People are leaving now who've never even done half of the service we done and leaving with a lot more money. OK money's not everything but they're coming out with things that people worked for years ago. They're coming out with the pension scheme that the likes of all of us put in. We didn't get much, coming out. They could have give a little bit more. They're giving pounds now to people to get rid of them, buying them off and this is wrong.

We had no choice, we had to go. Not only me. Dozens and dozens. I think they could have give a bit more. My pension is nothing compared to some of the girls I know who've only given 25 years there. They're getting the same as me or perhaps a little bit more , and when I look back at some of the old ones. . . There's people there, Bill Smith and them, they do 51 years, they started at 14. Men worked longer, they come out with nothing. I always think that they could give people of 80, make their lives a little bit more comfortable. That's how I feel. We go to see a woman of 80-odd and when she first left she only got £1.50 a week pension. I know money wasn't the same then, but don't you think they could go and say, "Here you are", but they don't look at it like that. I don't think they look after the pensioners as they should do, really.

I don't miss being there. No not really, no. I miss all the fun and all the larks. Don't miss it at all, never have done. I do see the girls and all that and in a way, I like to see the girls. I think that if they had something - I know they've got clubs but it's not my type of company; I shouldn't say that, but if they'd done something different people could have met up. They're changing a little bit now, once every year you get a little letter, we're having a get-together and are you coming or are you not. And it's rubbish. It's just like people go and have a cup of tea and that's it. You've been and tried it and that's it. I don't know, why go all the way there on the bus? And they send it out for half five of an evening, you know, till such a time.

I don't know about old age pensioners on the streets; I know it's not late for some but it is if they come from away, you know when it's dark and that. You think everybody's got a car. They don't think of them going on the bus or that so now quite a lot of them back here left, they didn't like it. No bugger turns up. My brother-in-law went once and he said to me "You missed a good night there, we had a smashing singer and they give us all a parcel". Don't you think they could give the pensioners a parcel? They could give some kind of help to some people. . . the waste they throw out and everything, they could give them a parcel. A gesture. But you've got to be 80 years old.

One time, when people died, I know it sounds soft but when people died, they used to come and say "So and so's died, would you like to go to the funeral?" That all went on. Then it all stopped. I think it's awful really, when people have given their service to the firm and that, they don't want to know. After forty years' service quite a lot of people, and there are a lot about, could do with a little help living in the times we live in now.

Richard Podmore
D.O.B. 24.4.09

Carton Maker
Worked in Levers
1924-1975

I started work at Stork Margarine in 1924. I was in the box shop there and then transferred after 18 months to the printing department at Lever Brothers. The box shop is where they make wooden boxes for the margarine. I was transferred into the carton department at Lever Brothers. I served my time there for five years as a carton maker, although I did do a bit of printing later on. We were more or less making the forms up for the cartons to be punched out on , making the forms up and setting the blades into them. Like a wooden box cut to the shape of a carton, and the knives have got to be fitted around the wooden box, and a cylinder runs over it and cuts the carton out, anything from six to 99. In the case of one carton it was a triangular carton, years and years ago. It was for something called "Snowfruit" which was like a sort of ice cream, it was a triangular icy block. There were 99 blades on one sheet which punched it out. We used to do 60 million of those cartons at one time.

I had the opportunity to go to Levers when I was 15 years old. My brother was in that department and he spoke for me to the Manager of the printing. I managed to get a job as an apprentice in there and it wasn't easy in those days even to get apprenticeships. I didn't fancy Cammel Lairds at all. I wasn't the build for a Cammel Lairds job anyway. I wasn't much good at lifting. I was living in Port Sunlight, only five minutes to work from where I lived in Port Sunlight, Greendale Road. Levers at Port Sunlight had a very good name in those days, very good. Anybody that used to work there was really working for a lifetime, that's what I did anyway.

I preferred the carton side of the work , I only ever did that. I went into the printing department for a short time, they needed men there and I was transferred there for about 12 months running printing machines, but only on the smaller side, I wasn't doing any critical work or anything like that, just running what they used to call the 'Shamnon' line which printed and cut out the cartons at the same time. I was on one of those mostly. But when the time came to go back to the carton side of it I was quite happy to go back. I was quite happy there. I worked in that department and that was the only department I worked in. It was my life's work in there, for 51-52 years. In the printing room .I was quite happy there.

My boss was an old chap named Mr. Calvert. His son was a supervisor in there as well, after his father, when his father retired. He took over for a while. He was an understanding man , he spoke to you in a decent manner, that kind of thing. Not particularly bossy in any respect.

There was one Manager I didn't like, I wasn't particularly keen on him, that's all I'm going to say about that. But I won't mention names. His attitude and his manner , he wasn't a popular man. He was the opposite of Mr. Calvert . He came about three-quarters of the way through my work there. Then he moved elsewhere. There was a sigh of relief then, not just from me but as much from all of the workers in general. If anybody hears this they will know exactly who I am talking about. But there weren't many bad fellows I came across during my working life anyway.

The best thing about Levers was the way we were treated ; we always got fair wages, and good hours. There was no problem working at Lever's if you behaved yourself and did what you were supposed to do.

My home was with my parents at 44 Greendale Road where I was born and then we moved up to 73 Greendale Road when I was about five. My dad had been a Lever man for 42 years. He came from Crosfields in Warrington and transferred to Lever Brothers. He was transferred from Warrington to Lever Brothers, one of the first men to work in there actually, in the soapery. They were all Lever houses in Port Sunlight then. Not now but then. They had very nominal rents. We paid only half a crown a week, rent or something like that. I ended up in a Lever House too when I got married. I had a house in Crossways I think it was called , in Bromborough and I stayed there, but not for very long. Then my elder brother advised me to go in for my own house so we decided on this one. I bought this house for £675. Today I suppose it's worth around £60,000. We've had this house for over 60 years.

It's hard to talk about some things like when people had accidents, but I saw one chap in the printing room, he had his arm off, carelessness I suppose. There were one or two had fingers and that damaged. I suppose they got compensation of some kind, I'm not too clear about that. The fellow that had his arm off didn't ever come back, but fellows that had slight accidents would carry on with the machines. They were always strict on that kind of thing, guards and things like that, but fellows never used to put the guards on when they should have done. Lever Brothers were always keen on safety.

In 1923, I can just remember that, there was a big strike. No it was about 1926, in the General Strike. I don't know if all of them in Levers went on strike, some of them came out but not all of them. I don't know why , it's too far back for me. I was an apprentice then so it was all right for me to go into work but I can remember it vaguely, you know, people standing outside the gate, that sort of thing . There was no chanting or anything like that , no, not so much in those days. Not as strong as it is now. But Levers always paid - they'd go out on strike although Lever Bros. were probably paying the correct wages as the union defined it in those days. They always paid union rates. Apart from that there were very few strikes indeed

I've no regrets about being there, or for so long. I'm quite happy with my pension, the pension that I get. I've got a good pension, and I've never had any worries in that respect. I've been retired 21-22 years now and my wife died on 16th of last July in Clatterbridge Hospital and we were both well kept by Lever Bros. If I had to do it all over again, starting in 1924, as a young boy, 14 or 15 years old, the way things were then, I'd probably do it again. I think so. I only went to an ordinary school , Church Drive School , and didn't have any special education or anything like that. I was quite happy there. I don't think I'd change anything about it.

But today, I'm finished now, I can't work. They've got machines to do it. Much better and quicker. I think if I was looking for a job today it would be in the electrical side, computers or radio and television. I've always been interested in that kind of thing. You can see that, with this T.V here and the Stereo I've got. Lever Brothers? There wouldn't be any point in working there again now , because they don't do my kind of work anymore. . . well you could serve your time there as an electrician, I suppose. I mean, it's not the same now, is it?

I don't think it's on the same level as it was when I started work there. It's gone down a little bit since then. There's nowhere near the number of employees there. There were thousands of girls there when I worked there. There were thousands of them when I was a kid. They used to come on a special train into Port Sunlight Station, most of those girls came from Rock Ferry or Liverpool, I don't know. But I only lived five minutes away, right opposite the Bridge Inn , Ellens Lane, so I walked to work. They didn't have cars then like they've got now you know, cars were few and far between.

I should think they're still one of the best firms you can work for, if you are able to get a job there these days, because the amount of people they employ now is very small to what it used to be. So I suppose in one way you'd be lucky to get a job there now .There's different machinery now and they've cut out labour haven't they? They've cut down on the labour..... computers, chips, all these kinds of thing have ruined the working man's way of life haven't they, really? I think that's a sad thing. I don't see what they're going to do about it. I can't see any way there's going to be full employment again.

The way the village is now, selling houses and that, well, it comes with the times. I'm not happy about it, but it's a sign of the times. Everyone is after money these days . I go up to the churchyard every fortnight to see the wife's grave. She was buried in the churchyard. When I walk through the place now, it's still a nice village isn't it? One of the nicest villages there is.

I went to Church Drive School, my wife was in Church Drive School. I joined the choir in the church and went from Church Drive School into Lever Brothers until I finished. I used to play billiards in the Men's Club , it was always billiards in those day, not snooker, I used to enjoy that . That was before I married . I was a member of the U.C.F for a while , the United Comrades Federation, because I helped to build a railway in the Far East during the war, I was away for over four years , but I don't like talking about that .

All my life I've been part of Port Sunlight, kind of thing. They do have things for the pensioners I believe, but I've never seen anybody really since I left. Nobody's been near me. I'm not really bothered. I'm quite happy, as long as they send me my pension.

Port Sunlight Old Boys Football Team 1933-34

Ken Hughes
D.O.B. 1.6.45

H.G.V. Driver
Worked in Levers
1969-1989

I started in 1969 at S.P.D Liverpool. In Sefton Street Liverpool, S.P.D stood for Speedy Prompt Delivery, which was the carrying company for all of Unilever products form Margarine, Soap Powder, Birds Eye Frozen foods, Walls Ice cream, Kimberly Clark Toilet Rolls, Gibbs toothpaste, deodorants, Bachelor's foods, tinned peas, all Unilever products. We generally delivered to all the shops, supermarkets, warehouses throughout Merseyside, which included Wigan, St Helens, Warrington as far as Runcorn, Wrexham and right around, and that was just S.P.D. Liverpool area, we had one in virtually every major city in the country and that was S.P.D.

I was going in there, and I was put with another driver to learn the routes. I had to literally walk in and stand round like a dummy, until the supervisor form the warehouse came up and asked me who I was and I told him I was starting.

"What's your name?" .... and then, OK , you're with that driver. I literally walked over and was introduced, I was told that I was going to be second man. He just said that this is the area we are going to do and that all this stuff here was going to be delivered. I'd never done van work before or anything like it, because I was a mechanic, fully qualified mechanic, and when we went out and I really enjoyed it, it was something completely different and you were meeting people.

I went there for the money. When I was working as a mechanic the money was terrible, it was honestly. I was getting engaged and this job was advertised, so I put in for it and I got it, whether it was because I lived here in Port Sunlight in my Dad's house, because my dad worked for Lever Brothers, whether it was that I don't know, but I hope that I got the job on my own merits.

S.P.D was a fantastic organisation to work for.It was a Unilever company. They were, a fabulous firm to work for, very caring in every way.

Levers were a really caring company in those days. I can only go on my father, he was Levers through and through , you could have broken him in half like a bar of rock, and he'd have had Levers printed all the way through him. You couldn't say a word against Lever Brothers, you couldn't, there would be a holy row if you did. Then they were a family company, a good 95% of the people who lived in the village worked for the company then. They were a very caring company then. That's how I thought about things when I started with S.P.D. Because I thought , well you know, these are great, a fantastic firm to work for, my dad was always building Lever Brothers up so I thought well, they must be exactly the same.

I got promoted onto the heavy haulage, by which I mean the artics, and we did warehouse work and I really enjoyed the night work, I worked days and nights for about eight years and that was the job I really loved. I'd take the night trunk down to Bristol, and the day work was mainly warehouses in the way of Asda and Sainsbury's main warehouse. Asda was to individual shops, Kwik Save was Kwik Save Warehouse, we never went to their stores. But that was the job I really loved.

We were away in places, saw places, going down from places here to Birmingham, to Bristol, up to Carlisle over to Leeds and Hull, go to Northampton, Leicester, you were just on the road. It's hard to say really, perhaps if you talk to ex- H.G.V. drivers of around 15 to 20 years ago , they would say it was fantastic, no hassle, not like it is now, it was great, it was honestly.

It had bad times too. I never forget this one job. I was told I had to go down to the docks and had a load of bags Levers had received, some powder of some description, off one of the ships that were coming from abroad, where I don't know. Well it was up by Seaforth I had to take these bags, so I got up there, got into the docks, and then you always had a heck of a job getting into the docks, because it was always "what's for me ?" ... know what I mean ?

So I had to go in and find the ships, go up and see the purser I think. I told him I had a load of bags there. He said ... O.K. throw them on the quay. I thought O.K. fine.

So I came off the ship, and the van was just full of these bags.

As I was just throwing them off pulling them up, a docker came along and asked me what I was doing. I said well I have been told to stack them here. Alright then he says, carry on, but they might have to be moved after , so if you're still here you'll have to move them.

After about an hour, hour and a half, just as I had finished, the chargehand/supervisor came over and said .... Oh no , you can't leave them there, They have to go on the pallets over there. So I got some of the pallets, I thought four would be enough. Now in that one and a half hours rats had appeared, God knows where from, in the bags and there was I moving them. Well that was it, I was in that wagon, away I was gone, I just froze, no way was I touching. On my way out I told this fella, "there's rats round there mister."

He said " there's rats all over the docks, you get used to it !"

I told him I was sorry for leaving this job , but I couldn't handle that. I went. I didn't even get a signature or anything for the bags. It was a terrible place. I'd never seen anything like it in my life.

My boss at S.P.D. was a good man , but I just can't remember his name. He was one of the nicest fellas you could ever wish to meet, I can picture him now, I wish to goodness I could remember his name, because he was fantastic. He was from Formby and had only been in S.P.D. Liverpool for about two years. Any problems you had it was "come on in son" it was always son, for everyone, in the whole place. "Come on in son and let's talk about it." If he could do anything to help, he would do it.

You had other bosses, later in Levers, that were very different to that style though. One I remember was a guy called Johnson. He was one of the managers that saw the rapid demise of the transport section in Levers. He thought he was the bees knees in every respect. Started in the offices, graduated to under manager in No.5 warehouse, then he became transport manager. Now a great many of our managers had never had any transport experience at all, they just didn't have a clue of what the job entailed. His way of putting things was just to get out and do it, as if we were the only vehicles on the road. There was no such thing as hold ups or queues as far as he was concerned, which of course was a load of rubbish.

They did have motorways then and like now they were bad. The M5, M6, M62 did have accidents and queues to contend with, you did have bad weather to contend with, but such things never came into his vocabulary for want of a better way of putting it. Why did you have a delay here or there he'd say, and as far as he was concerned all these little wrinkles that the job had never existed and shouldn't exist. But I just couldn't get on with him.

My worst memory of driving for Levers was a suicide. I was coming back from Bristol on the M5 round the Worcester area. It's the only area on the M5 that has a wall on each side. He just jumped over the wall and walked out in front of the van and that was that. Of course we stopped which we had to.

There were four wagons all told , one that hit him and three that ran over him, so you can imagine the mess.

I'd still go back to it though. Definitely. No doubt I would do it again. All in all we had the bad times and the good. But I will say that in Levers, it was only the last three or four years that it started to get uncomfortable. We had to start to realise it may be the downfall of a lot of sections in Lever Brothers, but all in all I enjoyed every minute of it. If it was back to what it used to be, and I had the chance to go back, I would , definitely. I've no regrets about working there in my time. You enjoyed your job, you knew you would enjoy it every day , because there was a great bunch of lads there.

Today it's a ruthless company. The lads in there now are so unsettled, they just don't know where they are , they haven't a clue where they stand anymore.

Val Button
D.O.B. 7.4.45

Machine Operator
Worked in Levers
1972-present

My first day was the most terrifying experience of my life. I'd never worked in a factory before and I remember . . . in those days we were only ever taken on on a six week basis, just given six weeks' work, but there was also an agreement then with the unions that anyone that was kept on after 12 weeks was made permanent. The majority of women never got finished up. They went there on a 6 weeks basis but at that time everyone was more or less kept on permanently. My idea was that I was only going there for 6 weeks and I've been there now for 23 years.

I walked in and the chargehand just said "Oh yeah, you go over on line 5 and make boxes." I didn't have a clue how to make a box; I wasn't shown how to make a box. I got on the line and said to the nearest girl to me.... will you show me how to do this? She said "You don't know how to make a box - we're going to have a good night here with this one." And that was it; there was no training or anything in those days. You just had to get in and get on with it, you know. That was my first day, thrown in at the deep end.

Funnily enough I was only there a couple of weeks and I ended up, because I was so nervous, I had to go to the doctors. He prescribed me some tablets for nerves which I'd never had before and I was allergic to them. So I was there for two weeks and off for the next two weeks!

When I went back, I went to the chargehand and he said "Oh, you're going to stay this time are you?" So I said well I have been really ill, I've still got the rash. She said "Get down to the surgery and have it recorded that it had nothing to do with the liquid that you're working on." That was my start there. After that, I was fine.

Most women were in the same boat. We used to have casual labour a few years after I started, who did come for 12 weeks and who were finished up after 12 weeks because of this agreement we had, but they'd finish them up for a couple of weeks and then bring them back again. But that gap in between meant that they didn't have to make them permanent. I was terrified because all I'd ever done was work in an office . I'd worked in Bibbys in Liverpool in the accounts office but having had two children, like, it was more convenient . My husband used to finish at 4.30 from Laird's so I'd pick him up and he'd drop me straight at work for 5 p.m. because I used to do the 5 till 10 shift.

Sometimes you wonder "what am I doing here? but when you've got two small kids and you're sort of struggling to make ends meet (we were buying our first house) you thought well , I've got a job, I've got to get on with it.

It was a case of seeing what jobs were going and it was, as I say, the evening shift suited me because it meant that Gerry could look after the kids and I was there through the day, he was there in the evening. It was the convenience of it, plus the money was good. It's always been good money at Lever's.

Funnily enough, when I left school I went to Lever's for an interview, straight from school, to work in the offices at Lever's, and I also went for an interview to work at Bibby's. I got the letter from Bibby's to start there on the Monday. I started work on the Monday and on the Tuesday I got a letter from Lever's to say I had a job there. But being a bit young, coming from school, I wouldn't go in and say I'd made a mistake, I didn't want to start at Bibby's and then leave and say I was going to Lever's. So in a way I regretted not going there but . . . it's always been in the background, it's a local company isn't it?

In those days, before I went there, I thought it sounded a good company to work for. Probably different ideas because it wasn't a factory I was looking for, I'd always worked in an office, so there was that side of it. And it was a bit of a shock to my system when I went into the factory for the first time. I remember me mum saying "You won't stick factory work, you've never done it", you know, but it worked out and the atmosphere there was good in those days, you could have a good laugh and go in and really forget the work itself because you would have a good laugh with everybody.

I've moved on since, but I was doing that sort of work right up until 3 years ago, but I've gone into the quality section now, so it's not as strenuous, it's more mental work. I was an operator on the line and became unit controller over the machine - I advanced to that level, but then with the new agreement, Horizon 2000, once that came out, unit controllers were pushed to one side anyway, we were all equal on machines and back to square one, if you like, without anybody actually being over the machine.

I think the job I'm doing now is a better job for me. It's more interesting, I'm my own boss although I've got bosses over me but I'm allowed to get on with it. I just enjoy doing it; it's not as strenuous - busy, interesting, but not as strenuous as being on the machines. Actually, the job I do is over the effluent in No 4 factory, trying to control the effluent, analysing it, analysing the water coming out of No 4 factory into the river, and also collecting samples down at the river to make sure there's no waste going out there, and contacting the River Authority and that sort of thing, but also costing up the amount of effluent we're producing in the factory and sort of organising groups to try and combat the amount we're producing really. Sometimes you hear about Levers polluting the river , but it's not us. That's LIL, which is Lever Industrial, it's not Lever's Port Sunlight. Lever's Port Sunlight have got an excellent record, you know, it's very, very rare that we break any records or limits going into the river. LIL is the next factory over and this is what's been in the news recently. It's not Lever's, it's LIL.

Mind you , I've had some terrible jobs over the years too. I think probably the most monotonous job was standing for hours on end washing labels off bottles that had come back contaminated and things like that. Just monotonous, boring work. Over the years we've done a lot of heavy lifting jobs, stacking on the end of a machine. Even there, over the years, they've been pretty fair. I had ten years as shop steward, fighting the cause for the women, you know. But although we've always fought against women stacking down, it got to a point where they gave an agreement where two women would stack instead of one man, so we got sort of halfway there but it was still hard work if you had to go on stacking as it was heavy.

We don't have stacking anymore, it's all automatic, done by the palletiser, It's been like that for about ten years or so now, I would think. What happened with the part-time women, our particular group (I worked in No 1 liquids for fifteen years) and we had hundreds of part-time women. When I went there I think there was about 270 part-time women in No 1, and we had lots of changes really - they decided that - maybe because we've got more active female shop stewards who started shouting for the rights of women and what we should and shouldn't be doing for women .

We screamed and shouted so much we ended up having equal opportunities come in and we started then - where we'd accepted maybe over the years that women did the lower graded jobs and the men's jobs were the unit controller sort of element of it. We were seen as the packers and the ones that threw the bottles on the felt and went in, had a natter, did the mundane jobs and went home again.

We started looking for better things for the women, and I think from then, to be honest, the part-timers' days were numbered. The company didn't like it very much. Although we did get certain better jobs and I was fortunate to get one of them, I think it was done as a token gesture, it wasn't done because we were as good as everybody else and they started by altering our shifts - we used to do 5 hours shifts; they cut it down to 4, the reason being it covered a relay situation, so that we didn't have so many differences to the men, the men that were on shifts.

So then we worked 6 to 10, 10 to 2, 2 to 6 and we fitted in with the relay. That was the excuse, but at the same time we lost 5 hours' work a week and lost 5 hours' pay. We got token gestures there. Then they brought in this early retirement and they made it 55 for women and 60 for men and the majority of the part-time women that were working there then were in the older bracket because they'd been there for a long time and it wiped out a large cut of the part-time women workers there. Once again, we started kicking up, saying that this was unfair, it was supposed to be equal opportunities blah, blah, blah, and at that time, legislation come out from Europe and this legislation was passed to say that it had to be equal, so although a load of women had already left and there was nothing you could do about that, then it was made 60 for both.

So a load of part-time women were wiped out there. Then the next move was to take us all from this No 1 area and put all part-time women in one area, which was then called New Products. Lots of reasons came from the company as to why they wanted us down there and there was a lot of bitterness from the women because we'd worked for No 1 for fifteen years, a long time, and then just to be chucked out. But we went down into this new area and were there for 5 years and we enjoyed it in the end because it was a niche for ourselves, doing the same sort of work, we took the machines down with us from No 1. We had men stacking down at the end of the line there, so that was going back then, so they were still stacking down up to five years ago in that room, but they were all slow speed machines in the New Products room.

New Products was a bit of a farce because we were told that it was a new product area which would handle small tonnage's of new products coming in, and we actually took machines down with us from No 1 and we produced Comfort and Stergene, the same products. So all this talk about us going down there to handle new products was a farce. We did do a couple of odd bits and bobs. One machine that came in there which we called Thomas the Tank, which started making the cartons of Comfort - that was a new invention. It was still Comfort but it was a new innovation into Lever's and we handled that well (well, we thought so anyway) and got it well under way, but then liquids was going to No 4, so Thomas the Tank Engine went there.

Eventually they closed New Products down and put us all into Pears, which was No 2 factory at Lever's, but the working life for that plant was only another 12 months, so after 12 months that room closed down and we could legally be made redundant. So the whole cycle, as I see it, was just a way of getting rid of the part-time women. There's no part-time women on site at all. When we left Pears it was a case of you went full-time, which was shift work and the majority of women couldn't do shift work, they had family commitments and everything else. Either that or there's no job for you. So the bulk of part-time women left two years ago.

I think where bosses are concerned you remember each one, don't you, for different things. I mean one sticks in my mind. When I first went to Lever's we had two chargehands: one of them, Jessie Parker , was a real Sergeant major and you were terrified of her. If she said jump you jumped, she was that sort of person. But at that time, I suppose I'd been there two years, and my mum got terminal cancer and I went to hospital to see her and I went back to work from there. But while I was at the hospital, my mum was only 50, and they told us there was no hope, like, and I went back there, to Lever's, and that woman looked after me - she was a tartar to work for, but from that day on she really looked after me, and you don't forget things like that, do you? I still laugh and joke with one of them now, Alan Millington, he used to be a shift leader down in No 1 and he's now our Safety Officer where I am now, and we have quite a good rapport between us and we talk about all our yesterdays and laugh and joke, and I still remember him in that way, you know.

I can't say I've ever sort of had a major problem with any boss. . . we had some niggles if you like , in that because we were static part-time, we had three supervisors, not one specific one, because the supervisors were on shift work and the problem we had with them was that one would see a thing one way and the next one would see it totally different and you'd be working to a certain method and be quite happy with it and then the next week a different shift supervisor would come in and his ideas were totally different and whereas it suited you before he come in, you'd think Oh God, why doesn't he do it this way, it's much better, but they all had their own ideas and didn't want it to be altered, they wanted it that way and that's the way it was done. And in those days you didn't argue.

I became a shop steward mainly because I wanted to know what was going on, and just feel that we can get out there and speak up for people. You never feel that people are putting the true voice forward, do you, you know, and the shop stewards that we had at the time, to me, weren't committed and I thought well if they're going to be my shop steward, I want them to get in there and fight about what's going on and come back and tell me, and I didn't think they were doing it so I thought well the best way to do it is to do it myself., not that I wanted to rebel or anything like that. I could always compromise with most people and see two sides of every story, and that's a sign of a good shop steward in my way of thinking. So that's what I did.

The best thing about working for Levers was probably the people that you worked with, not the job itself. There was nothing brilliant about the job, it was mundane and hard going and heavy work. It was heavy going but the people themselves made it. You always got the characters didn't you? You'd go in and if you had problems at home you could go in there, have a moan for five minutes and then switch off and forget about it and get on with it, sort of thing, have a natter and forget what was going on outside. Yes, I think the people were probably the best thing I remember.

There was one girl there who just lived a totally different life to everybody else - she'd think - every man in the room was terrified of her, you know, it was a conquest. New men came in they had to be hers and the things she got up to was nobody's business. I said if she wrote a book I'd be the first one to buy it!

It was just - you couldn't say, I can't put my finger on it right this minute, but different things they'd come out with, you know. Things like: one time, we packed a load of Sunlight Lemon Liquid and instead of yellow caps they put red caps on, which are the Squeezy Liquid's (they hadn't changed them over) and all these pallets were frozen (frozen means they can't go out of the factory) so there was about eight of us working in pairs and one was putting the yellow caps on and one was taking the red caps off and we were working through these pallets. I'm standing next to another two girls, one of them was the standing chargehand. I thought, they've been on the same box for the last half hour. We're working our fingers to the bone and they haven't moved a box yet, what a cheek! And then I looked, there's one taking red caps off and the other one mistakenly putting red caps back on and they're doing the same box on and on and on . . .!

We had another girl there who didn't even think she was funny, and the things she used to come out with were so dry, in the end you'd have to stop yourself laughing at her because she thought you were getting at her. She was telling us about working in a pickle factory in Rock Ferry, and she had a step-mother. She was saying she got this step-mother a job in the pickle factory and she warned all the girls before she came there "Whatever you do, no dirty jokes, no wisecracks because the stepmother is really stern".

It was the worst thing she could have done, because from the time her stepmother walked in this factory they were shoving gherkins on the seat for her to sit on etc. but she told this story and we were saying, yeah, yeah. That programme was on the telly at the time about a pickle factory with Jimmy Jewell. One of the girls looked up and said ..... any minute now you'll be telling us your a relation of Jimmy Jewell and she said "Well actually, our so and so was in service to them". This was the sort of thing that would come out all the time.

It's funny actually as for 19 years I worked with women and the women were really segregated from the men. The man was the unit controller, the domineering man on the line. If he saw you talking he'd come down on you like a ton of bricks and the back labourer was the man but the rest of the crew were women. The Back labourer looked after the back end of the machine - the unit controller would put front labels in and watch the caps and everything else and control the crew. The back labourer would put back labels into the machine and tidy round the back end of the machine.

So the two main jobs on the line were always the men and the rest was women. So you went for your tea and meal breaks all women together, the men went at different times because they were on shifts. So you were really segregated. For 19 years I'd worked with women and when I went to work in No 4, I chose to try shift work rather than lose my job altogether and all of a sudden I went in and there was only myself and another girl on the shift, the rest were men. It was really awful. I'd worked with men, the odd one, and being a shop steward had worked with all the male stewards and that sort of thing, but to go down there on that shift work and walk in , and I was going on nights for the first time.

I was on a machine in the middle of the room, and the other girl was off on holiday and I looked round the room and thought, What the hell am I doing here? Why should I be on nights at this stage in my life? I'd always worked part-time. But once I'd got used to the men and working with them, it was no different to working with women as well. The only thing you miss, obviously, you can discuss women's things with women, can't you? You did miss that, and going in and having a natter about women's problems and things like this and comparing notes, sort of thing, but it was more of a challenge once you went on shift.

You'd get this feeling that it didn't matter what had to be done, you had to do it, because you were being paid exactly the same as that man was being paid. In your own mind you wouldn't let it be seen that they were helping you because you knew what they'd be thinking. You were always trying to prove yourself. Even when we got these unit controller's jobs when we were on part-time you felt you had to prove that you could do that job. Where it was expected from a man you had to prove that you could do it. It's always been like that there.

I did have some problems with some of the men over gradings though because I was a higher grade than most of the men because I'd got that unit controller's job and we had a maintained rate agreement in there, that once you'd got that rate you wouldn't lose it. As long as the company had asked you to do that job, you'd never lose that rate, so I was always one grade higher than the lads. In my nature, I was able to laugh it off and instead of antagonising me, I was sort of saying to them well it's up to you to start looking out for yourself and trying to upgrade yourself and once you got there you wouldn't want to lose it either. So I was all right on that score and having had years of experience as a unit controller, I was as good as the next man, so I didn't feel too threatened
.

In fact it was funny when I first went down to No 4 as they didn't know me down there, I'd never worked in No 4 before. They'd taken a load of new lads on and they put me on a machine after a couple of weeks with a complete crew of new lads and they were really good to me. This young lad came up and was saying, "When you throw the bottles out, Val, you break the box. Put them down this way. You don't mind me telling you do you?" I said no. I got talking to him later on and

I said something about being a shop steward for ten years. He said "Oh where was this?"

I said "here."

"What do you mean, here?"

I said " I've been a shop steward here for ten years. "

"Here ? " "Where? "

"In No 1."

He said "How long have you worked here?"

" 21 years."

He said "My God I feel such a fool, I've been telling you how to break boxes down and you've been here 21 years !"

But we became good friends after that. But I wasn't sorry to come off the shop floor, I must admit, and come on to quality. It's hard working the factory.

One lad lost the top of his finger because he put his hand in the machine, his own fault actually, when it was running. There was another funny story. We went on a first aid course. We were always a bit put out because we never thought we were used properly as first aiders, you know. Someone on the next line would have an accident and they were whizzed to surgery before you were even informed about it. Well when I did my first aid course, it used to be a full week then, and Sister Campbell, the factory Nurse, came on that course as a student, because she wanted to know what we were being taught, so she could assess what she could leave to us and what she couldn't leave to us, sort of thing. She was good on that and I got very friendly with Sister Campbell.

This particular night the chargehand that was on at the time was a first aider and he knew me as I used to go on the courses with him. One of the girls had fallen off a steep pallet at the end of the machine and as she went she heard a bang, so she said, and she was stretched out on the floor, so we decided that she'd broken her ankle or she'd possibly broken her ankle, and we got pallet boards and rags and we taped her right up to her thigh. First Aid guidelines says keep the person cool and laugh and joke with them to take their mind off things , so we were having a laugh with her.

They sent for the security men to take her to the health centre. Anyway, he came in with a chair and he saw the way she was strapped up and run back out and brought a stretcher. It was Christmas time, and Lever's used to give us a turkey every Christmas and it was the night we were collecting our turkeys. So I'm saying to the security man,

"Whatever happens, make sure she gets her turkey tonight, don't let her go home without the turkey."

So he took her to the health centre and we were all concerned thinking she's broken her ankle. Anyway when we finished at 10 o'clock we all went down to the main canteen to get our turkeys and the security man was down there giving the turkeys out. I went up to him and said "Can you tell me how the girl was that went to the health centre?" He said "Why, who wants to know?" I said, well actually, I'm the first aider that strapped her up. He said "Oh I see, ... well she's just left." I said "What do you mean she's just left?" He said "Oh she's been in to collect her turkey." I said "What about her broken ankle?" He said "No, what she'd done was she'd torn the tendons so they'd strapped her all up and she tripped over to get her turkey." We'd done her up like a dog's dinner! Sister Campbell would have gone nuts .

Over the years there was quite a bit of what you might call 'industrial unrest'. Mainly really with the part-time women having our hours cut. The problem with it is that as a group, you're a group of a union if you like. The representation , branch officials and such have got to represent the whole group or section. We started off with 270 women in the room compared to 50 men and after the early retirement thing came in, we ended up as approximately 70-100 women and 120 men. So all of a sudden from being the majority of women, you're now a minority and slowly eroded until they don't exist any more. So when we had our hours cut it was a big thing to us, we'd lost five hours, and we actually had to go in - we were called together as a group of stewards to work out how the men were going to work the extra overtime to cover the hours that the women were losing.

Right away we started screaming saying well hang on a minute. Women have never worked overtime in No 1, it just wasn't done. Men worked overtime in four hour blocks. We said there's no way you're going to allow these men to work over until we get our five hours back. So there was plenty of to-ing and and fro-ing. Then a lot of women became quite happy with the hours they were working, now they didn't want overtime. So we came to a compromise that for every two men that worked, one woman would work. Bearing in mind that when a woman worked, because she was only on part-time, she got paid normal rate for it. If a man worked over he got time and a half. But because we had to also watch that the company didn't use all women, we had to come to this compromise that we worked out how many women wanted the overtime and how many men wanted the overtime, and we come up with a stipulation in our factory anyway that for every two men that worked, one woman would work.

There were all sorts of things that went on. As I say, we started fighting for women to become unit controllers and to have higher graded jobs and things like this. Women were always second class citizens in Lever's. You come off the line for a "spell", a break away from the machine for five minutes. The women would sneak in the toilets and have a smoke behind the closed doors - the men would go and sit in the mess room. That was accepted. Even the women would accept it. You'd never see them go in and rebel. It just wasn't done. The men were allowed to go in there because they were full-time. The part-time women just weren't allowed. You'd go in the cloakroom and all stand in a little group talking and this Jessie Parker would come in and someone would give a whisper "Here's Jessie!" and everybody would fly into the toilets and get about 3 or 4 women in the toilet. She'd be on her knees looking under the door to see how many pairs of feet were there! We got that wise to it we'd be standing on the toilet so she couldn't see us! Then I'd come out and say "I don't know what I'm locking myself in here for, I don't even smoke!" But I had a sort of rapport going with her and I'd come out and say "You've got me terrified of you, I'm shutting myself away in there and I don't even smoke!" She'd just give me a backhander.

But I liked it, working there. As I say I got to like the independence of being out to work and it's an escape route if you like from being at home all day when you've got kids. Just to get out for a few hours and of course it eased all the worries. A few extra bob coming into the house. With Lairds you always had that worry over your head, was it going to close. How much longer would it last.

My only regret is that working the way we did, we girls worked 5-10 in the evening, you miss the kids growing up. It wasn't until I left that and went onto an afternoon shift and my kids were Gerald 14, Linda 11, so they'd grown up and I'd missed it. They were at school all day and I'd take them to school, pick them up from school, give them their tea and then go to work. If you like, it wasn't till you actually came off the shift that you realised . . . They were in bed when I got back. All the days that they were in the Oval Athletics, running, Gerry saw to all that, where I'd have liked to have done that. So you realise what you miss when it's too late, sort of thing.

I'd always like to work, I'm that type of person, I like my independence and I hate money worries, so you would do it. But I've no regrets at being at Lever's. Times have changed over the years. I'd say I'm one of the fortunate ones because the job I'm doing now I enjoy and the people I'm working with I get on well with. I'm not competing all the time for brownie points. On the shop floor it's dog eat dog now and back-stabbing all the time. There's redundancies and when they do things like issue a list twelve months ago with 120 names on and say we don't think you'll be required in your job, and then it comes out you've got two choices. If you sign to say that you want to go, we'll keep you on till next March, but if you don't sign, you leave in October. So they'd sign. So it's voluntary redundancy. But it's not, it's just another way of doing it, it makes the company look good doesn't it. It makes them look as though everyone who's gone has gone voluntarily. No enforced redundancies. They sign to say we'll like to leave next March. They'd get an extra six months work out of them.

Levers isn't the caring place it once was. They still profess to be a caring company but I think anyone going in to it would probably have totally different views to me, but people starting there now have had spells of being on the dole, working for contractors with no terms and conditions, so they think the terms and conditions that are there now are brilliant. So if you spoke to one of the new lads he'd probably tell you it's the best thing since sliced bread. But having been there such a long time, and knowing the conditions that we had. They're so different.

We lost a lot when Horizon 2000 came in I can tell you. And your life's not your own. They'd worked shifts in the past but you could pick and choose. If you didn't want to work over you didn't work. Now on this scheme, the lads owe the company hours and I think they're trying to change it again now because the company are not happy with Horizon 2000 either and these self-managing teams are alleviating a lot of the problems because they're covering each other, working out their own hours, whether they need to go in and when they don't need to go in. So they haven't got the same grouse as a shift leader coming out saying "You're working till 6 o'clock tonight, you're working Sunday like it or not. You'll be on 12 hour nights all next week." You couldn't argue against it. They're trying to alleviate it and the crews are trying to work their own hours out.

When I think back to the terms and conditions we lost, we know them, but the new people coming in don't. So there's the difference, and I think that as well . . . maybe it's not true but to my way of thinking all the people that were told in this lot now that they could be losing their jobs are people who've been there a longer period and know what went on before Horizon 2000 came in.

It was a way of bringing in different working practices, getting rid of old agreements and starting afresh. I don't think it's just particular to Lever's. I think they were the starter of the local factories. Gerry works at Octel now as a shop steward and he comes home and tells me about talks they're having and they're easing into it. I've got a brother at Quest and they're easing into it. It's all this working annual hours rather than working weekly Monday to Friday. It means they can call on you anytime and the company are saving millions of pounds.

On the USDAW wage bill when they first come into it, right away we could work out what the wage bill was the year before for USDAW members and what it was going to be, because they had assessed that there were no extras, no overtime, no call out pay, no specialities on top, just basic money. They saved £3,000,000 in the first year, so it was a money saving gimmick for them put over in such a way that like it or not it was coming in. They gave us so much notice of it coming in and if we didn't sign it then everybody on site would be issued with a new contract of employment. In other words, we either went in on a negotiating basis, still there able to negotiate, or they would just shut everyone down. You didn't have an option really. But it hasn't worked out and the company don't like it for several reasons. It's working out that it throws up 390 surplus hours a year and they're not reaping them all back. If you like, they are paying money for nothing. But at the same time, the people are not happy because of the pattern of work they're having to do. They're working Saturday morning for basic rate, working Sunday for basic rate. It just hasn't worked out .

I wouldn't like to be starting again now, not in the environment they work in there. It's so totally different to what we had. It's the atmosphere, it's not there. My saying at the moment is that I'm just glad I'm at the end of an era rather than at the beginning of it, because I've seen the good times there. I mean, don't get me wrong, when we talk about good times we had to work mighty hard, and we worked in the time when a supervisor said jump you jumped.

What they're going into now is all this self-managing teams and they've all got to be their own bosses and they're all so clever and technical and heaven knows what, but they've lost a lot of it on the way. Although you had the supervisors before and at the end of the day he had the last say and all that, you respected them for it. You knew what they were. That was their position and you knew how to work with them. But now, it's so airey fairy. I wouldn't start there again now. I wouldn't recommend anybody to go there because the atmosphere is so different today.

The 10th Company Consultative Conference, for workforce and management representatives, at Port Sunlight in 1985. Val Button is on the second to back row, fourth from left but partly hidden. Eric Coates and Frank Birks are here too.

Francis Mckeown
D.O.B. 7.11.04

Chimney Sweep
Worked in Levers
1939-1968

I went broke and had to find myself a job and I got a job in there for the war. When the war was over you were finished, you were out. It was on my record what I did before I went to Sunlight. There were 11 of us to be booted out but I was one of four that they kept on, because I'd done some chimney sweeping before. They asked me if I'd like to stay on to do their chimneys so I said yes I would but that the wages were no good. They wouldn't pay the craftsmen's wages. They took me in from the oil pumper yard.

I was an oil pumper , emptying and filling oil tanks. You see when the war was over it turned out that I'd been working under the Government - margarine works, food lark. So anyway I decided to take it on, and that was it. I never did get a tradesman's wages.

I had nowhere else to look except Levers ,Cammell Lairds was no bloody good to me. What would I do at Cammell Laird's? The only skills I had were hard work. I was put on the road at 17 years old in Liverpool after two years of training as a chimney sweep and the police took me off the road because it was against the Health Act - Child Labour. It wasn't allowed until you were 18. So the boss employed an unemployed fitter from Cammell Laird's until I was 18 to beat the cops. So I worked there right up to 1929. The 1926 coal strike knocked the arse out of everything in the way of chimneys. Every office in Liverpool had a fireplace. Then they got gas fires. I was there until 1929. I knew it was sinking and chucked it and started on my own in Birkenhead , sweeping where I could. Then I went bust and I had to find work.

In the meantime I'd run a business. I had a contract for MS Public Houses on Merseyside. I had the North Western Hotel, Lime Street, Liverpool and in 1939 I lost both of them. They told me that they'd only got 14 pubs on this side of the water and the least they could do was Liverpool work for Liverpool people. That was helpful, wasn't it? Then the next thing was they closed the North Western Hotel down so that was it.

As for Levers I hated the sight of the bloody place because when I was 15 I got the sack from the Post Office, I was a telegraph lad at Birkenhead Post Office. And my mother said to go to Sunlight to find work. I went with another lad the same age as me and I said to him,

"Do you want to work at Sunlight?" and he said he didn't.

I said "I'm bloody sure, I don't ".

I had a couple of sisters working there and they stank of soap and scent. We went to Wood Street, where they took you on and sat on a form and they gave you a paper. There was an old fella on the front and the procedure was that you filled in the paper, what you were and what you weren't and then the old fella would call you out. I said to my mate, the next time he calls out, dive out with your paper and chance it and we'll get chased. The next thing was the old fella called this kid out and my mate bounced out with his paper. He was chased back again. Not long after the same thing happened with me. So he brought the pair of us out, rolled the paper up, told us how bad we were and never to show our faces near Lever Brothers. That was it. We were happy - We'd been for a job but didn't get it so that's when I went for the sweeping lark.

Years later, because of circumstances, I found myself having to go back there. I hated the sight of the bloody gates. I thought that I was in jail, and listening to the backchat of the bosses, the chargehands, all that caper, "Come here you, I want you". It's a wonder I didn't kill some of them.

My first day was simple fright. It was fright. They had me buggering about here, there and everywhere. The chargehand said "Go there" so I went, I wasn't there long and he said "Come with me". We were walking along and I asked him if they still had the suggestion system here. He told me they did so I asked where I could I get a form. He said "I'll get you a form but what is it?" I said that my suggestion was they cut me up in little bloody pieces so I could be in half a dozen different places at once. He should have sacked me then but he apologised and said it was hard lines.

The next thing was they put me in an old pumper filling wagon. A string of wagons came in and he showed me what to do. Anyhow, the man doing it collapsed and they carted him away. The boss came and said he had been taken to hospital and wouldn't be coming back again. Then he asked me if it was alright that I fill the wagons up. Well, you know the size of the wagons and with not being in industry before, I thought "Does he think I'm going to do this on my own?"
I said "Get me a mate and I can".
So I got this mate and I took the place, with two shillings rise on my money, from the man who snuffed it.

I was moved from the oil pumping to Safe and Solvent Plant, the plant used to take the red out of the fat. The job was a reserved occupation but they didn't tell me that until after the war was over. I didn't know. Anyhow, that was it. Well the poison that they were using - Lystersol - you see the Fuller's Earth - the fuller's earth was the colour of dried cement but when it's in the tank with the oil it takes the red out.

I got three pounds 19 shillings and fourpence and that was shift work. For 48 hours a week. I was married with a kid , but there was no bloody chuck to buy was there? You helped yourself. As for thieving anything out of Sunlight, you'd be crucified unless you knew how to do it.

They couldn't pay the full wage because the sweeping was only done two days a week. Those two days were enough for anybody. On the other days I did other work, Drains, gutters, downspouts. I wouldn't be called a chimney sweep. I christened myself a flueologist.

Well I invented this flueologist though there is a word for a sweep which I didn't know, but I came to the estate yard and the fella who used to do the sweeping became my mate and the pair of us were going into the factory for something and I saw a lazy bastard coming along the other side of the road with a long white coat on, collar and tie and I said to this bloke, "Isn't that so and so over there?"
So he said "Yes, you do know him"
I said "I know him, the lazy bastard but what's he doing with a white coat on?" He told me that he'd just come back from London after doing a course for the new works council thing.
I said "What was the course?" and he told me it was psychology. So I said if he had the bloody cheek to call himself a psychologist I would call myself a flueologist and it stuck.

Once while I was on the oil pumping, there was a leak, the pipe was rubbing up against the tank and it wore a hole and when you pumped the fat was running down the side of the tank. So I asked the fitter what the chances were of the boilermaker fixing it. He said he'd fix it, and not to start the pump until one o'clock. At one o'clock, this lazy bastard, he was the boilermaker, he asked me what the trouble was.

I said "Look at the bloody trouble up there, the fat running down the side of the tank".

He said "Have it unshipped" and buggered off.

That means to take the pipe down, unhook it, bring it down and he'd come back and do it. So of course I started the job up again, the fitter came round and asked who'd come.

So we said "That lazy bastard".

The following day two more blokes came up, put a step ladder up and he wasn't there 10 minutes and the thing was going well.

The best job - there was no best job at Sunlight and as far as muck was concerned, the safe Plant was bloody rotten with muck, fat and poisons. There was nothing good in it. I could never say ......I'm looking forward to going today ... Oh Christ no. They'd try anything once. They weren't bloody human.

Before I went to work for them at all, a doctor recommended me to the matron at Sunlight Hospital and she asked if I might be interested in sweeping their place, and I thought "Christ I'm on my way to fame, Port Sunlight Hospital". I went to see her to arrange a day to start. I'd be there at six o'clock in the morning and I'd be there for three mornings. The first morning I arrived and the porter was there so I asked him where to start and he said he'd show me. So he took me in and there wasn't anything in the room, nothing. So I asked if they were having the painters in, so he said "No, why?".

So I asked him about all the furniture and he said it was all in the passage and that's what they always did. So that's how they were going on, emptied the sodden room of everything before the chimney was cleaned.

So anyhow every six months, she'd tell you the date for the next time round, the bill was six pounds and something for the three days, and I got the cheque from London. That was alright. Time went on and she phoned and said she'd like me to come along on such a day and I told her it was too early, it's not due. She said "I want you here". I thought I'd be doing them twice as often instead of once. I arrived and went through the performance. I was having a smoke and the two porters were sitting over there.

One fella said "It's hard lines on you mate, that it's your last trip".

I said "Why?"

He said that she had bought a kit of tools for them and from here on they had to do it now. I made the bill out, £12 odd and I sat at the phone waiting for her to tell me of the balls I'd made of the bill, but I never got a cough. They never did cough up

I was the first in Birkenhead with the black handled phone one instead of the two piece one. I waited for her to phone but there was nothing.

I made a name for myself in Sunlight, because I went into a house and there was only a table in the room, nothing else. I checked the chimney and the woman came in and asked me if I'd finished. I said "Yes". She looked at my mate, and then she paid 1s 6d for the chimney to be done. She said "You see those two 2-bob pieces on the table, that's what I pay a woman to wash this place out after these people have been here". So you can imagine the state of the place after her usual sweep.

It was left so clean that when I got back to Sunlight, the chargehand told me I was making a name for myself round there. I told him I'd made a name for myself years ago before I went to jail. He told me the matron wouldn't have me near the place.

I said "The cow". Of course the word went through anyway and I was ordered to the hospital. They had their own hospital then, the buildings still there at Pool Bank. I forget the matron's name now. I know there were two people at her funeral - I wasn't one of them. She kept out of my sight.

I was performing on the grate when the door opened and the tiles were that bloody polished it was more like a mirror. She came through the door and backed out. I got up from where I was and met her in the garden.

"Morning, Matron". What could she do? Then when they closed the hospital down and she went to live up somewhere there she sent one of the porters who used to run round after her to ask me would I do it. I said "What's wrong with the firm doing it?" Well wouldn't I do it privately so I thought I might as well.

The best boss I ever had was Mr. Borthwick. He was a gentleman for a start, and I wasn't used to two-bob things. There was another, I forget his name now. He liked his wallop. When we were working there on a Saturday he went for his dinner at 12 o'clock and at 3.30 he came through the gates again and said "Listen I'd like you to clock off at 5.00 and report to Bromborough Dock at 10.00". I said "Who's dropped dead?" Of course he was as drunk as a Fiddler's Fish.

Whale oil stank like hell. So I said to him "I don't want that bloody whale oil job, get some other gobshite to go".

So he come back pissed off and said "Clock off now and the see the manager Monday morning". Of course I buggered off. He wrote his death warrant, his evidence sort of thing, on the envelope and arrived on the Monday morning and you lined up for him to tell you where to go and what to do. I was supposed to be getting the sack.

Anyway I went up to the Mess Room to have a smoke and the fella who was looking after me said "For Christ's sake mate, put it out! You're in enough bloody trouble!"

I said "How do you mean I'm in enough trouble?"

He said "Well it's either so and so or so and so who's going to get the sack".

I said "I don't give a monkey's".

I finished my smoke and was waiting to see the foreman. As he came along I was down the steps and he was a bit deaf. When we turned up the road to go into the office, a couple of the lads on the other side waved to me and said "I don't want to do this to you". With him being deaf I let a bloody roar out so that he could hear it and so could the other two.

I said to the foreman "You're taking me to see a gentleman I should have seen six bloody months ago". The manager. We arrived , then knocked on his door and the foreman said "You wait there". I thought this was bloody funny. He was in there long enough and then he came out and said "Mr Borthwick will see you".

I went in and Borthwick said to me "I was very surprised when I was told there was a man to be brought up - you're one of a new intake, we recognise you via a small increase, but listen, you go back to work". I was delighted about that.

He said "On your way down see Mr Chesworth". So I went down, there was a girl there, I'd never seen her before.

I said "Where's Chesworth?"

She said "Who are you?"

I said "Francis McKeown"

She said "You're the one who's been causing all this trouble".

I said "What bloody trouble have I caused?" I'd caused no trouble.

I buggered off and going through the yard the foreman's mate said "How did you get on, Mac?"

I said "I've been promoted to Tommy Riley's assistant", because on the way down another boss had told me to report to Tommy Riley. Then I got the letter out, it was from Unilever London, it said I was drunk, and

I burnt it.

The worst boss was the Estate boss. I took my own tackle into Sunlight to do their sodden chimneys. They had a parcel of shite that I wouldn't have lit the fire with until they bought something for me.

Anyhow I hadn't been on the Estate for a month or so and the boss there called me into the office, he had a sheet of paper and he said "Wouldn't you call that a few day's work?"
I said "No, why?"
He said "I feel unsatisfied"
So I said "Listen, I've never been on the mat in my bloody life".
He said "You're not on the mat".
I said "What am I then, and another thing, this is no time to get at me. Twenty five past bloody five, I've got to get scrubbed".
Anyhow I was ready for chucking the job, he called me in again. I was supposed to have knocked a chimney pot off a house I'd never seen and was never on the list, I'd never even been there.
I said to the other fella, my mate Lee "I'm getting the bloody hell out of here".

So anyhow I wrote to the boss, Borthwick. I don't know where the bloody hell they'd got that from. Anyhow I wrote to Borthwick and told him I'd like to defend myself against the allegations. I wrote it out and read it out. Sealed it up, posted it, and the following day there was a notice on the office window "McKeown, Lee, the chargehand and the foreman - Manager's office, Thursday 8.30 a.m."

The chargehand was shaking like a leaf and he said "It's you who enquired about this enquiry so I'll leave it to you". So I told them in the first place that this was no nark, and all I wanted to know was if they'd not been satisfied with the work, or was the accusation about the amount of work I'd been doing. When they showed me the work list as like evidence, it was only one of the sheets. Where are the rest of them I asked ?

I'd been here, there and all over the bloody place, and those orders had come direct from the office. Then the panic started. They brought the fella in and asked him how long this had been going on. He said "It's always gone on".

So anyhow I said "All I'd like to know is do you want the chimneys in Port Sunlight to be swept clean as they should be or would you like me to revert back to the Sunlight system".
He said "The what?"
I said "the Sunlight system". He asked me explain that.

I said "I can't explain that properly but Dick Lee can tell you all about it".

He said, "We know nothing at all about the job". I told him about knocking a chimney pot off I'd never seen, they didn't like the new people I suppose, and then he said to the chargehand "Well what have you got to say about this?", and the gobshite said "Well I am his supervisor but I know nothing at all about his job".

So the boss said "This has gone on long enough, get back to work and I don't see why there can't be harmony in that little place of yours down there". We were going out and he told the foreman to stay. So after we'd gone Borthwick must have said to him why didn't he let me come and see him in the first place, why didn't he use his loaf. We had to carry on with the work, we had to go to Bromborough and when we came back there was a notice on every bloody doings in the yard .... As and from .... whatever date .....anybody desiring to see the Manager can do so through the usual channels.

There were no bloody strikes in Sunlight. There was a strike years ago but I wasn't there then. Billy Lever didn't like strikes. That's why we had two shillings a week extra. The wages when Sunlight opened were two bob more than labourers outside. Railway men got 18 shillings a week, Cammell Lairds 18 shillings a week, Corporation 18 shillings a week. Billy kicked off here with £1.00 a week. That was to button you up to no strikes. Same with the houses.

I took a Lever house about 1957, I was grateful for that. It was handy. I didn't have to carry my loot down to New Ferry. Loot? Well the wages were no good, so it had to be topped up with something, coal, wood, anything that was knocking about. Nobody was bloody thieving, we were just topping the money up. Increasing the revenue.

This wasn't the first house they put me in, I was with the family before this place, first at 49 Corniche Road then number three Corniche Road. This place is only a dump.

The biggest laugh I had in my life was when they made me a workers representative. I had posters, the typist in the office would type them out for me. The last meeting I was at was a lot of bloody hooey. They were chewing the fat over somebody's suggestion that there should be a clock in the Mess Room and the Chairman said "McKeown have you anything to say?" I said "I've been watching that clock for about three weeks". The bloody clock had been in three weeks.

The fella who had suggested the clock, a fella belonging to the estate, was supposed to get a prize so I said to him "Your clock's organised so you're due for a £1.00". He said "Is that right?" I said "Well I put it to them that you did it, I'm working hard for you bloody people, you know. I get no soddin £1.00". When it came up for the £1.00, they said they'd decided on ten shillings. I said "I object to that for a start". They said that it was only a small thing, but I said that it didn't matter because it was supposed to be £1.00 for a suggestion. He got the £1.00.

I only did it for fun. Well there was no fun anywhere else. My chargehand said to me one day I had to report to the Fire Station at 2.00 p.m. because they were having some sort of demonstration. I went up to the Fire Station, I was there on my own. They got a big tray out with fat, oil and petrol on it, set fire to it and explained to me how it could be put out. I learned a lot there. I was supposed to pass that on to the people I represented. I was to explain to them how to put it out. I went straight home and on the Monday the supervisor asked me how I'd got on at the Fire Station. I told him it was very interesting, I'd enjoyed every minute of it. He said "Listen, I believe that thing only went on until 2.30 p.m." I said "Yes, that's right". He said "But you never came back". I said "What the bloody hell would I be coming back for? I went straight to my home to get down on paper all what I'd been taught to be passed on to my men".

If I had to do it again I would . I wouldn't have missed that because I was educated in it, in the system. It was an experience. I was educated in it. It's like a sect, it won't be like that now because there's only a handful in the place. I wouldn't work there again the way it is now though, would I buggery.

I saw him once, Old Billy Lever. my father took me down to Birkenhead Park, in the '14 war, to see an inspection of troops. Billy Lever was doing the inspection. He formed the 13th Cheshire's. I'd be about 10 and that was the only time I saw him. Sunlight itself was a bog and his father had told him to keep his eyes skinned for a spec where he could build a factory. I think it was about a quarter of a million they spent on it.

He built houses for the workers and he won a big prize. He wanted the lot. He bought the island of Lewis and he told the Scots what he was going to do and they told him to piss off but that was the foundation of Macfisheries. Billy Lever, his idea was alright, because he was going to organise where you got the fish, where you cooked it, where you canned it, the lot, but the powers that be wouldn't have it.

It's not a Company at all today, not a firm like it was. Levers have got nothing to do with it. It's one bloody conglomerate. The Dutch pulled them out of the shit years ago.

I haven't seen much of the place of late but they seem to keep going. There's no humanity in it as I see it. I've no regrets, I hold the record, the youngest chimney sweep ever, and the oldest. I cleaned my last chimney when I was 87. Not for Levers though . No, for myself.

Francis Mckeown the 'Village ' Chimney Sweep

Harry Williams
D.O.B. 2.2.16

Clerk of Works
Worked in Levers
1931-1978

I started at Lever Brothers in 1931 and I finished work actually with Unilever London. I worked for three companies, Lever Brothers from 1931 to 1960, Unilever Merseyside till I was 57, about 1971, so I worked 1971 to 1978 for Unilever London. As I am a pensioner now on our record I finished with Unilever London not with Lever Brothers.

I was 15 years old when I started as an office boy in the what was called the Repairs Department - it was Bromborough Port Construction Company it was then, but it was part of Lever Brothers and it was on the New Chester Road where that white building is - where the UML offices are now - by the Village Hotel. There was a footbridge over into the factory there - so I was the messenger/office boy and I was there about a year and then they wanted the apprentices. What they did then, Levers put on the notice board - "The following apprentices are required" they wanted a printer, a mechanical engineer, a plumber and a joiners apprentice. Well my grandad, he was the first foreman joiner that old Lever employed here .He died in 1901. My dad worked there from 1889 to 1945.

So I applied for the apprentice joiners job, I went to the staff training college which is now the men's club and there were 203 boys applying for 4 apprenticeships. so they gave us a simple test - the three R's - reading, writing and arithmetic. The subject of the essay we had to write on was the downfall of democracy. I wrote that I didn't believe in the downfall of democracy - as far as I was concerned - a democratic government had to prevail - anyway - I wrote a good essay and I got an interview - I think they interviewed about 32 boys.

I went then to the Staff Training Manager and the Service Manager - they call them a Personnel Manager now - a fellow named Waddle. He said well - your English paper lad is better than anybody else's, the tense is right and the sense is right and it's an excellent paper but I think you have applied for the wrong apprenticeship. I said what do you mean Mr Waddle? He said well you should have applied to be a printer we'd be pleased for you to be a printer. I said I don't want to be a printer - I want to be a joiner. Printer is a better trade than a joiner he said. I said if I'd wanted to be a printer I would have applied for it. Well why do you want to be a joiner? I said well my granddad was a joiner there have been joiners in our family since time immemorial - I just want to be a joiner. Oh all right lad he said.

Well then I got another interview then - I was sent over there to see the Building Manager. He was a new fella that had come since when I first started and they sent four for the apprentice plumbers job and four for the apprentice joiners job. Well what he did then - he said well look laddy - your a bit small to be a joiner - you couldn't carry a purlin up a ladder on a roof - I said that's not joinery that's carpentry - I want to work in a joiners shop making furniture, doors, windows, stairs - that's joinering. Oh, he said - well how do you know about that? I said well I do, I know about that. So he said well if you weren't successful in having a joiners apprenticeship would you consider having a plumbers apprenticeship. I said no I wouldn't. He said - well it would be better than being a labourer. I said I know - but I'd sooner try Lairds or somewhere, you know. I just want to be a joiner.

So what he did - he told us after - he offered the four lads who applied for the joiners job - if you couldn't be a joiner would you be a plumber and three said yes, and the four lads who applied for the plumbers job he said well if you couldn't be a plumber would you be a joiner and three said yes and one said no - a fella named Ken Hooton - he's still alive - he's 79 he lives in Kings Road. So he gave us a brown envelope sealed with a real seal on it - you know - a wax seal. So he took us to the staff training college and he lined 16 lads across the hall like that and old Knox put his pince-nez glasses on and said the following boys have been successful in getting apprenticeships. Harry Williams, the joiner and a fella named Cliff was next to me with his tears coming down his face. So I got a trade then. They sent for you then and said - you've got to go to night school three nights a week and we'll give you Saturday morning to do your homework. Because they worked Saturday mornings in those days you see. You would go the staff training college and the old Clerk of Works, old Roberts, he helped you with your homework. He had all the apprentices there and then until you were 18 - from 16 to 18 they sent you to the staff training college two hours in the morning and two hours in the afternoon and they gave you an insight into book-keeping and all that sort of thing. Of course if you didn't attend night school you know, they took the apprenticeship off you.

I expected the sack when I was 21 because you served your time and they gave you three months as a journeyman and they they gave you your cards. Fortunately for me they had woodturnering as a separate trade from joining all together, its part of a woodworking machinist's job as a specialist. Well they never had enough woodturnery to keep a full time woodturner so they had an old man called John McEwan and he could do woodturning and joinering as well - he served his time at Prices years ago. Well what happened then - he was coming near 65 so he had to retire well they thought it would a be good idea to train an apprentice to do the woodturning you see, so they got hold of Jimmy McCormick - he was the eldest lad - he'd be about 20 - so old McEwan said well he wouldn't make a wood turner. So then they tried Emlyn Roberts - he was about 19 and he said - no - he wouldn't make a wood turner. Then they tried Ken Humphries - he was about 18 - he said - I don't think he'd be very good. So then they tried me - Ginger they called me then. I was 17 and a half, and he said oh Ginger will be alright - he'll make a woodturner. So he taught me how to do all this you see.

But when I look back, he didn't want to leave work you see - he went to Lairds after but they kept him on until I was 21 - you see what I mean - there was a method in his madness. I was extended from 17-1/2 he got me another 3-1/2 years didn't he. He was turned 68 when he finished, well when I came out of my time - instead of getting the sack - they sent for me, the managers, and said well look your a good lad and if you keep your nose clean you've got a regular job here. So that's what happened and so I got kept on. I was the first apprentice joiner to be kept on this century

It was excellent because they had what they called merit money - whether it was fair or unfair - I got 4 bob and when I came out of my time the wages was £3 17s 6d a week and 4 bob merit money made £4 1s 6d didn't it. Well that was good, I mean some only got 2 bob some got nothing but I got 4 bob. And of course the thing was the first year I gave my mother £2 a week lodging money and so it meant, and I only paid half a crown income tax so the rest was mine and if your had a pound in your pocket like you were well off. Well you could buy at Burtons in the sale for 37s 6d a blue serge suite with a waistcoat and all. So I was happy with the firm, everybody wanted to work for Levers. Because they paid over the odds you see, you were getting a pound a week more even than they were getting at Lairds.

I think he paid over the odds so he could get the cream workers - he didn't suffer fools lightly did Billy Lever. You see this is the point and they were strong disciplinarians. If you smoked you got fired out - you didn't even get a second chance. You got stopped. And so he paid over the odds compared to other people around because he could get good people - my only criticism now at the back end of my life is this - that in those days - if you got a house on the village it made you even more secure in your job. Because if I lived on the village and you didn't and there was going to be redundancies well if Lever was paying me £4 a week and he was getting 10 bob back in rent he was only paying me £3 10s and you 4 quid if you lived in a council house so people were encouraged to live here. Well now, all these years on with the Rent Act as it is they keep putting the rent up every two years. I mean these people could have bought a house, I could have bought a house long ago but I stayed here and looked after my aged parents you see. I've lived here since 1930. I was born in Wood Street right opposite the factory - number 35 Wood Street.

It did, oh absolutely, no doubt about that - no question about that. It was a job and the house went together didn't it. I mean in as much as it was a tied cottage - you had to work for him to live here. If you lost your job you lost your home. You were happy to do it because it was security, there was unemployment in the 1930's like there is now - a hell of a lot of it, and since that time - and then what happened to me again - the war came and of course we all had to register for military service for the Army, Navy or Air Force which we did. I went with this fella Billy Spencer to join the Navy. Well it was after Dunkirk and of course they sent us back and said well you go back and get on with your work we don't want you in the forces for now. And then the Germans started bombing us and what they did then, they had what they called the Ministry of Labour, National Service officer - well of course he came to Levers and said I want a lot of joiners to go around and fix bombed and damaged property because it was all hanging in bits all over the place so we were doing dead shores and flying shores and all sorts. So they sent for us here....

So we went to the Council for about 18 weeks and they said well our service counted just the same at Levers as if we had gone in the forces. Well then the bombing stopped after I don't know how many weeks. Quite a number of weeks, well we had to report back to the National Service Officer. Well then he said well look we are not sending you back to Levers, some went to Lairds and I went - they wanted a man at Fawcett Preston at Bromborough. Seven days a week - 12 hours a day - 12 hours a night - the other old fella there he came from Liverpool and he didn't want to do any night work. So I worked for a year - 12 hours 7 til 7 on nights. And then I worked for 2 years 6 nights and just had a Saturday off and then after that it was 5 nights.

And then the Germans gave up and the people got released from the forces so Levers of course applied back for all the fella's. Some went to Martin Herns some went to Lairds - I went there - some went to Fennyborough in Leicester - I don't know what they were doing there it was a munitions place of some sort. Or some went to Grayson Rollos & Clovers - but we were all sent to jobs which were in what they called a reserved occupation work of national importance. And what happened then the Manpower boards in 43 used to come around and they'd interview you you see. Well I'd go in and say well OK Mr Williams - they had all these dossiers - you've been directed by the Ministry you go back to work. Well other fella's had gone on a course like, dilutees, making shelves, - well they substituted them with women and they just put one skilled man in charge of six women so they got called up. So I didn't go in the forces.

I came back after the war and in the joiners shop I did all the setting out. I got 3 ha'pence an hour for that. So every job they made in the joiners shop I had to mark it out - if it was a staircase, or a window frame or whatever I set it out and ordered the timber and give it to another fella to make it. So I got 3 ha'pence for that. And then the old foreman dropped dead in 1948 so they made the chargehand Jack Youd the foreman and I was temporary chargehand at the time. Then they put on a test, they changed the name of chargehand to supervisor and wanted 15 fella's to go on a management course, a supervisors course to Burton Manor College in 1948.

So they test you and there were over 600 people applied for it and I was one of them. Again it was a test - a simple test and I passed that, then we had a group discussion. The group discussion was they put you behind a screen and there were 4 adjudicators outside - you didn't have a name only a number and the subject to discuss was "is the only guarantee of good quality work a fat pay packet?" And of course a lot of them said it was. I said I didn't think so - I said I thought the first thing was the proper industrial relations and mutual trust between the employer and the employee was the first thing for a guarantee of good quality work. And people to be happy knowing they were working for a fair employer and for the employer to also know that he could rely on the employee who appreciated the fact that he was permanent. And of course there were eight there and I won that one and they were down to 33 then. They sent me through to see the Personnel Director and the Technical Director.

They asked me then would I consider having a job outside the building trade - I said well I would but if you think I was intelligent enough or smart enough to train I would and then they said - well we think you are very intelligent man Mr Williams - don't you? And I said you will have to try a bit harder than that if you want to get inside Harry Williams I'm not falling for that one. Have you got any questions you want to ask us. I said Yes. Could you let me know as soon as possible because this has been going on for about three months this. And they said yes they would. And of course I got in the 15 and I went off to Burton College I remember the 15 fellas'. There were 3 electricians.

Then they were going to build a new oil mill out at Bromborough - The New Oil Mill they called it. A ground nut processing factory and they had a resident engineer who came from the Admiralty a fella named Sidney Wood and he wanted a Clerk of Works so they sent me down there - by that time I had a Higher National Certificate, City & Guilds of London Institute and so I applied then for the part two of the Institute of Clerk of Works and sat that and passed it and they promoted me to Clerk of Works and I was Clerk of Works then for many years.

The best job inasmuch as I gained the most experience because it was reclaimed land that we were building on we built a factory, an office block, a canteen, a laboratory and it was reclaimed land so it was piled and on top of the piles there were pile caps and beams. I had never seen anything like that - the experience was gained there and also we built a cellar in the office block. Well we had to bring in a dewatering plant to lower the water level so that we could make the mill so I got a lot of experience there. And the fella that I worked with - Sidney Wood, whose now in Canada, who still writes to me even at Christmas - he's 84 now - he was a gentleman, he was a lovely fella Sid and we got on like a house on fire. We used to go along and play Mahjong with him and he left and went to Canada. So I think it was the best job inasmuch as for the two years I was there I got a wealth of experience that I hadn't got otherwise I was limited to carpentry and joinery work wasn't I. There I learned all about piles, brickwork, plastering, steelframe building and reinforced concrete frame buildings and it was marvellous really.

The worst job we ever had was erecting blackout in the factory just before the war broke out and taking it down afterwards. Because all we had to stand on was one plank on a cripple in a roof truss, it was like a wooden frame and just a plank. You only had one plank to stand on and you had to take all this blackout down - it was bloody dangerous - there was no question about that. They wanted all hands on deck to get it all down and get the factory repainted and cleaned up after the war because it had done nothing for six years you see. That was about the worst job I ever had.

I didn't enjoy it but I really had got to do it because I worked in the joiners shop and used to get all dry soap and everything all in the room and all over you, you came home looking like a miner. So I suppose they expected you to go in at the weekend. They didn't force you to go Levers, but they moreorless expected you to go so I went and did that. Again I was glad of the money you know, the wife had just come out of the forces and we were just getting on our feet so, that was about the lousiest job.

Once I was looking after a job which is now Unilever Research up there, and it was what they call the Motor Vehicle Repair Department (MVR). We were modernising the building and there was a firm, industrial engineering and they had some steel people, they were doing some alterations to the steel in the roof and a man named Bert Harrison, he fell from this tie beam and he fell on his head - he only fell 11 feet but there was a hole in his head like a cricket ball - he was dead. Terrible it was, I'll never forget that, he was just dead on the floor.

When I was an apprentice joiner we had a foreman named Dave Marsh he came from Gossage you see in 1932. Lever's bought Gossages out from Widnes. We closed them and brought them here and he came and another fella came - Jack Youd - he's since died - he was a joiner. And Dave Marsh was an excellent fella and he was a good geometrician and he was interested in you. You know, he made you sharpen your tools properly and he was really interested and if you were interested in night school, he would give you jobs which involved geometry and circle work and stuff like that. So he was a great boss he was - no question - but he dropped dead.

So after that I went with Sidney Wood then after that on the Oil Mill and he was great and of course his boss was a fella named Eddie Scott who was quite a nice fella - he was a gentleman but he was bit distant from the staff you know he was nice but he was a bit aloof - he was a nice guy - you could talk to him. Then of course after that I was more or less my own boss then. What I did, I worked in conjunction with architects and structural engineers and surveyors but what they did then if Unilever wanted a building built, they drew their own specification up the Engineering Division what they wanted and then they put all the drawings and specifications and they put it out to national contractors you see. The power station at Bromborough - well Jarvis' did that. Well then the cheapest contractor did the job. Well then I'd go on site then and see that the job was build according to the drawings and the specification and all to the British Standard and qualifications I used to have to look after drains work in conjunction with the local authority and everybody.

Eric Scott retired and a little fella got the job named Alan Stealy. Now he was a wash out. What he had done, he had gained a paper qualification somewhere but practical experience he had none at all. Although he got the job and if you wanted him to know anything or discuss anything with you he'd say well that's your line of country, you can deal with that. He didn't want to know, all as he was interested in was how much they were paying him and where he was, he was a bluffer really.

So in the end what happened when I was transferred to London, I was going everywhere, Windsor, Yarmouth and Aberdeen and Spalding. I met a lot of nice people on those trips but I was living out of a suitcase and what Unilever did in those days in the 1970's we had a Labour government in and for every pound they spent they got a pound off the government. So if a project cost £9m they paid £4.5m and the government paid £4.5m and it took over a lot of firms.

I was tired of living away and living out of a suitcase and going away on a Monday morning and coming back on Friday night and so, Well I said I want to retire because what I've got left of my life I want to spend with my wife. I wanted to go the next August so I'll give them a years notice. Stealy wasn't happy. He stormed out of the office and rang up somebody in London who was his boss and he came back with my report and on the back it had typed on it "I understand that my retirement is entirely voluntary and against the wishes of my section. And that means, he said that you will lose twelve and a half percent on your pension. I said, well if that's the thanks after 47 years and the way I've pulled my weight here, I said give us it I'll sign it. Then I signed it.

Well I went then to Craven Arms and that was the last job I did, Craven Arms near Church Stretton. They bought a small firm out - Chucky Chickens and then called it Midland Poultry Holdings - quite a big job . I went there for a year.

I went there in about the September, and in the April they sent me a note saying let me have a formal note indicating your intention of terminating your service with the company next August. So I just wrote back and thanked him for the letter and said implement the necessary procedure for my retirement as verbally agreed last August.

Then I sat down and wrote to Ken Durham who was the Chairman of Unilever and I said that I had been with the company for 47 years, my father had been with them for 56 years, me wife had served them as a nursing sister for 28 years and I felt that a company as enlightened as Unilever for the sake of posterity would have a better method of a man completing his life's work and being compelled to resign. I got a very nice letter back from Ken Durham saying that he would get the Personnel Director to look into it for me and he did. And they found out that in 47 years, all that I lost was 41 days work and he wrote back and said that in view of my excellent service the Chief Engineer of Unilever felt that I should be invited to retire at the company's request and the favourable difference that it would make to me would be that I would lose nothing on my pension

Then, he came to me, Stealy and said you can have a party in the Bridge Inn for twelve, and I said well there's fifteeen of us in the section so I'll invite the other three myself and pay for them myself. He said you can't do that. He said you've got to have twelve, I said well I'll have none, it's as simple as that. If I can't have the fifteen, I'll have none, it's that easy. So he goes back again and he says, okay, they say you can have the fifteen, so I had the fifteen.

I was the shop steward at one time before the war. And what Levers had, apart from the shop stewards was what they called joint consultation. Every department had joint consultation and what you did, you put fella's up and they were democratically elected. They hadn't necessarily got to be the trade union representative, they hadn't go to be the shop steward, just someone in the department and you voted for them and each department had 4 members, and they had a meeting once a month with the management to discuss any problems and snags which may arise you see. Once every three months they had a co-ordinating council of all the departments representatives together at Hulme Hall and that helped both the employer and the employee to solve a lot of problems. An Levers also used to invite all the trade union delegates every year to a party and Levers always paid a few bob over the union rate - they always did that. It kept them sweet.

Once, when I was a shop steward, the joiners were in dispute with the people at Lairds you see. And Leo McCree, he went round the factory and wanted us to walk out, well we wouldn't do that. He said well these are your brothers, and we said we know they are but we've no complaint with Levers so there is no reason why we should walk out of Levers if you can't come to some compromise with Lairds. So they wouldn't do it. The only strike I remember at Levers was the General Strike in 1926 I was only 10 then.

I definitely would do it all again, because the amenities were good, the opportunities with the Staff Training College and everything else was good, there's no question about that.

It's different now though. I have a nephew down in south Wales and he has a sweet stall in Aberdare market and he's doing very nicely. I think I would work for myself in this day and age and try to get my lad to work for himself or work for me.

My opinion of the Company today is that it's just as ruthless as any other company. Its only concerned about profitability and staying in the industrial war that they're in. They are in an industrial war with Proctor and Gamble and all the other industrial nations on the face of the earth so they are just as ruthless as them. They've got to be to survive.

I think that they do try Unilever, when you are 75 they send you £4 and a card . It used to be £3 and did it for 10 years and they gave them a Boots certificate for £3 and I used to give them £3 and claim the money back. About 50 people used to go round and knock on doors saying I've come from Levers Pension Association, they said well your not interested in me because they put my rent up every two years. Which when they amended the Rent Act you see, this UML company they never failed to do it you see. Course this time their asking for £3 but their only getting £2 because its under the control the Rent Officer. They used to have a pensioners dinner every year. Van den Bergs kept it up the longest, but they've dropped all that now, there's nothing like that any more.

One lad I know I stayed with his mum and dad, and his dad died so his mother became the first successor. So she has a regulated tenancy controlled by a Rent Officer and then his mother died and he's a fella of about 35 - 40. Well then Unilever said to him, well you can have the house for £40,000 or the rent's £45 per week. At that particular time I would be paying £20 per week. So he said well I haven't got £40,000 I'm out of work anyway and I couldn't pay £45 per week. Well you can apply then to the Housing Benefit. So he applied for Housing Benefit. The Local Authority and the government pay - he pays if you like £5 per week to quote a figure and they pay £40. Then at the end of the year it is only an assured tenancy. At the end of the day they come and say well the rent is now £55 per week and so it goes on.

Unilever want rid of these properties. Well they'd sell this village now if they could get a buyer but while they are tenanted they can't get anybody to buy the 300/400 houses that's left en-bloc because whose going to give them a few million quid for houses that are on a controlled rent. But they want rid of them you see because where Lever had this spirit, now it's an international company, there's no village attached to Birds Eye, or John Wests or Van den Bergs, or Unichema - they haven't got that bother have they. They don't want to be bothered - they want rid of it.

I love the village, the only regret, not for my part because I can afford to pay the rent, the only thing I feel is mean about it is that they encouraged people to live here, there are widows both sides of me, Tom died as a result of the war in '47 and his wife is crippled with arthritis completely, she only sleeps on the settee . Mary Willis next door too , they were encouraged to live here and they still put the rent up, they still want to put the rent up you know.

Unilever don't need that sort of money, you know. I mean they as young people could have bought properties but they chose to live here for the security and now, in their old age, in their middle 80's they are still asking. Course they have to get out if they say well this lady has to find £63 per month to add to her Unilever pension, (she doesn't get any pension) to pay the rent. I wrote to them about it, but I didn't get anywhere.

Even if you go and look at the war memorial now its green mouldy and there's graffitti on it. And every year we used to clean the bronze statue, there's none of that now.

The estate had their own painters, plumbers, they had everything. You got free maintenance on the property. You only had to ring up and it was done. In the olden days the outside of the property was painted every three years. And the inside was decorated every five. Well now, you're responsible for the inside, I built this kitchen myself in here. I'm responsible for the inside of the property and they paint the outside every 6 years and now our front doors gone rotten. They screwed a piece of plywood over it and painted it. But you could take them to task if they went over seven years. So they leave it to the very end. Next door they've had to replace windows and all sorts they've let them go for so long they've gone rotten.

Well I was happy there and I was contented and of course the wife had a good job, she was a nursing sister with them. It was a secure job. My brother was killed at 24 and my parents had difficulty in getting over that really. They were old, and my wife and I looked after them until they were both 87 and they are both buried over here with my brother.

My wife came from Kings Sutton in Oxfordshire and we looked after her parents and they were quite old when they died. But when I look around, since that time, I've been all around the world America, Fiji, Hong Kong, Tonga, Hawaii, Australia, New Zealand, Japan, China, India and in particular America, the wife and I with what skills we had could most probably have been better there than we did here. But there again you see we've had a wonderful life. It was a good social life here, there was contentment here, there was security here and above all there was a nice atmosphere in the village, you had a sense of belonging.

There was a sense of belonging to a worthwhile employer and a worthwhile society, there was this sense of belonging . There was this spirit.

Its gone now hasn't it. What they've done now you see, they've sold the village off, and the people who've come in are not taking part in the village activities any more. They just don't want to know and quite a lot of them are old people who have sold a property for £80,000 outside and bought one here for £50,000 and got £30,000 in the bank. So a lot of them don't take part in it and then and it's just died hasn't it. You see Port Sunlight had it's own football team, hockey team, cricket team. Well we used to play Unilever House, we'd go there and they'd come here but that's all gone by the board. Any industrial relations and the sense of belonging I was telling you about is just non existent any more. They just don't exist.

It's been deliberately snuffed out, in as much as costwise. For instance, Dorothy was a sister in charge of Van den Bergs surgery for 25 years. They had 4 nurses, a doctor, a dentist, a physiotherapist they had all that. Dorothy had a phone and the nurses could ring her up if they had a problem. They had all those amenities. At Port Sunlight you could have your teeth done, you could have your eyes done, you could have anything, but they have closed it all down. Van den Bergs now, where the wife was, where there were five of them, there is one State Registered Nurse there from about 8.30 till about 4.30 and if they have an accident they just bugger them off to the hospital. So they've just cut down you see

To my way of thinking, this is where we've gone wrong as a nation. The government and industry should have got round the table together and said well we're in this scrap - the same as we were in a fighting war, we are in an industrial war and the CBI and the government and the TUC they want to get down to brass tacks but they haven't done that. The Germans have, and the Japanese have but we haven't. Its true.

PORT SUNLIGHT,

CHESHIRE,

To Co Partners All   Nov 11 1912

My dear Co-Partners

I am writing you this short letter before leaving for the Congo so that it may be enclosed with the Special Co-Partners number of "Progress" for December and the report of a Co-Partner address I gave last Friday at Birmingham. It is just as true of our scheme of Co Partnership as it is of Co-Partnery in a Fishing boat that if we dont all work well together there will be none or very few fish Caught and consequently none there to divide and equally true that we cannot find room for learners on others or for passengers.

Copy of a letter from W.H. Lever to all Co-Partners in November 1912 .This copy belonged to Harry Williams's Grandfather

My dear Co-Partners , I am writing you this short letter before leaving for the Congo so that it may be enclosed with the special Co- Partners number of "Progress" for December and the report of a Co- Partner address I gave last Friday at Birmingham. It is just as true of our scheme of Co- Partnership as it is of Co- Partnery in a fishing boat that if we don't all work well together there will be none or very few fish caught and consequently none there to divide and equally true we cannot find room for learners or others or for passengers.

In payment of your dividends on your Co-Partnership Certificates this and for succeeding years you will receive as far as practicable Cumulative Preferred Ordinary Shares of £1 each in Lever Bros. Limited bearing interest a @ 5% which I hope you will keep as an investment. But if you must turn them into cash you can sell them through the employees savings bank on giving 24 hours notice to that effect and signing the necessary transfer forms the cash will then be ready for you to draw in full.

I most earnestly hope however that you will make a strong effort to keep them and become a shareholder in our company increasing each year. Yours Faithfully W H Lever

Maurice Brown
D.O.B. 14.06.29

Production Worker
Worked in Levers
1949-1989

I remember starting there in July 1949 and being interviewed by a man by the name of Bill Cooper who was the foreman in them days in toilet soaps. George Tasker who was the under manager and them asking us if we could stick the job working inside, most of us had just come out of the forces. Just come back into civvy street. They threw these questions and I said no, I don't think I ever will stick it because of the atmosphere, there's no bloody fresh air and the stink of perfume from the toilet soap department. But it just seemed to grow on you. As I say, after 40 years you became part of it.

I'd never worked in a factory before, I'd always worked outside before I went in the forces, and to come back and be closed in, make me do a twelve hour shift, we were when we started, 1949 they were just starting to wrap the soap again, wrap the products because it was never wrapped during the war because of the paper shortages. Of course we found ourselves working six twelve hour shifts, six twelve hour days and back in on the Sunday night for six twelve hour night shifts. You came home with about twelve guineas in your pocket. It wasn't bad money in 1949.

I went there mainly because my family had worked there all their lives. My grandfather, my father, I had three sisters working there at the same time, and a brother as well as uncles and aunties and quite a lot of people in the family worked there. They seemed to be doing alright out of it so that's why I opted to stay there. My opinion of the company was, there was always somebody sitting on your back, a chargehand or somebody sitting on your back. My first job was shovelling soap all day into a big hopper. Big lumps of it. It had been milled and had come through three sets of mills into bins and you'd shovel it and shovel it out of soap bins. The soap bins had half inch bolts sticking up in the bottom, and if you hit them with a shovel, you knew about it, you can't complain you know. Some of them had square wheels on, and trying to pull them around was some job, and woe betide you if you let the hopper go low because you'd lose the pressure on the plodder and it would have to be pressurised again.

The new soap chips get shovelled into it and there is a screw inside it, it's only a 16" diameter worm and it forces through a cold water chamber into a hot water chamber and then it binds itself together into a bar. Then it goes out onto a cutting machine which automatically cuts it into billets and then it was fed into a stamping machine and had the name stamped on it what ever it was, Knight's Castille, Lux or any of them.

I remember one fella losing all his fingers one morning in one of the soap mixers, took them straight off in one go....one Saturday morning. Actually how it happened, when I was working in number 4 toilet soap. They started the NSD up there (Non Soapy Detergent) department which was a new thing round about 1952 and they asked for a good nucleus of labour off the toilet soaps to start this plant up and it wasn't running right and it used to come back to us on overtime. Or maybe it must have been after 1952 because I was a chargehand. This particular fella I said, go back on your old job and within an hour, I was sitting in the office having a cup of tea with about six or seven other chargehands and supervisors and he walked in, somebody had put a tourniquet on his arm. I said "what's the matter?" Well, the lots gone, cut off.

How it happened, on the soap mixer, to open the door, it was on a screw, you turned the handle and the screw opened the door and the soap dropped down. On the end of the screw there was a collar secured by an Allen screw which had come off. He had put his hand through the guard, thought he had hold of the door to pull it on and his hand was actually in the mixer and it just chopped them off. A few people got the end of their finger off.... because the safety in those days wouldn't be what it is today.

In them days, in toilet soaps they used to do about 50 different brand names, and they used to do soap under licence for ICI, soap called Tetmosol, that's a short name, it was a very long name really, and that was mainly shipped out to New Zealand and Australia for the sheep farmers. They used to wash the dogs in it to get the sheep tics off them. That was made under licence for ICI and Cuticura was made under licence for the Proctor Drug Company .There were about 50 different lines, but now there is none of that; they just have about five main lines i.e.: Lifebuoy, Lux, Knights Castille, Shield and all these other ones are farmed out to third parties .

I stayed in No: 4 toilet soaps from '49 till about 1972. Then I moved up to No. 1 Liquids making plant where all the dishwashing liquids were made, fabric conditioners and all that lot. That's where I finished my time. I only worked in the two departments all the years I was there like. I think working in the liquids was a more satisfying job than the toilet soaps because in toilet soaps we had women under us. In the liquids making it was all male only staff. It was a better atmosphere working with an all male crew. The difference was, in the toilet soaps in it's hey day you could have as many as 120 people here on the shift and when I worked in the liquids making there were only eight people on a shift it was more sophisticated process. Of the two, the liquids making was the better job of the two. Anything was better than shovelling soap all day for twelve hours a bloody day.

If you behaved yourself, after twelve months you moved up a little bit, somebody left or somebody died and you got promoted a little bit along the line. They used to operate a job rate scheme in those days. The lowest job rate was two shillings a week, that was packing on the end of a line. Everybody got the same basic money. You were graded to a job rate scheme and the lowest was two shilling and the highest was twelve shillings but that was putting the ingredients in the soap, you know, the mixing of it, you had to have a little bit of knowledge about you. You could move up one niche. Then when I became chargehand it was twenty eight shillings a month the flat rate. So you were only getting sixteen shillings a week for being chargehand, above the highest paid operator. Sixteen shillings was a lot of money in those days. When I moved down here in 1954 into this house, in 1955 I think the wages then was only about twenty eight pound a week. The rent of this house was one pound fifty then.

I could have applied for a Lever house in the village, round the back end of the job it was known as the 'historical slum'. The only thing with a Lever house was that if you looked sideways at the boss you were out of a job and out of a house. Not only that, the smells round there, around the Sunlight village, not now, but they used to stink terrible from the factory, the smell. I didn't want one. My grandfather lived in one on the New Chester Road and I had relations living in the village but I've never fancied one. I wouldn't have liked to have been on the doorstep.

The chargehands job, it just grows on you - it's not a case of coping with the change, it's using one's own initiative and how you handle people. Obviously you went on training courses, there were plenty of courses to go on, you were trained to do the job. Bossing is an art, being a boss of any description, oh it is yeah, man management you could call it. Its horses for courses when you've got people under you and you don't break anyone's heart, you try to be human, but I'm afraid in the old days, I remember before the unfair dismissal act came in, people perhaps working on the mixers and they got affected by the perfume, they could get a rash on their hands. So they'd go to Lever's Health Centre and come back with a note saying this man must not work near the perfume near this or that and the boss used to say 'well I'm sorry, that's the only job I've got me old lad, go and get your coat on and when you get to the top call in the time office and your cards will be ready and that was it.

It hasn't always been a paradise, oh no. Like before the Safety at Work Act came in, you didn't get protective clothing. You know I worked outside and you made your own bits and pieces up with old sacks if it was raining to keep yourself dry, and you didn't get boots and all this but when the Safety at Work Act came in that's when all that changed the way we got treated.

As I moved into liquids making I only had a day work boss, there was only a boss who stayed till 5 o'clock. If I said to some of the fitters on nights, I want that done. And they've said, well your not qualified to tell me what to do, I'm a fitter. I said, look son, I'm Billy Lever after 5 o'clock, I'm Billy Lever himself, I said, and you leave that and get on that. And he'd tell me, well I'm not in the fitter's union, and you'd get all these silly little things coming up. I used to give them the option, either he could do it, or I'd call his boss and he could tell him to do it.

But thank God, I had a good working relationship with the trades, electricians and the fitters, had a good working relationship with them. Unfortunately one of the other chargehands didn't and he just couldn't get things done with them.

I had a few good bosses, Joe Gooch who I still see, he's 84 Joe, you should go and have a talk with him. I was with him on Tuesday night in the Lever Singers. I'm in that and there are a few of the old ones there. Trevor Roberts was the Works Safety Officer there, he's in the Lever Singers, he's 81 or 82, but still got his faculties, they're the people you should have gone talking to really, they are interesting people. Joe Gooch was alright, he was a very fair man. The last boss I had, Ted Balham, he was very fair. I had a good working relationship with both of them.

If you got a bad one, you just slowed down, you didn't give the extra two penn'orth did you. But it didn't worry me that, but we used to call some of them, we had nick-names for them, like 'the Drug Addict' when you've done that I've got some more for you'. They used to call me 'The Vicar' when I was chargehand. Eight hours with me, an eight hour shift with me and they were all on their knees.

It became a secure job as things went on. I can remember going back 30 years ago when I was on toilet soaps and I was off sick. I'd had quite a big operation. My own doctor said I think you should have a fortnight convalescence, I'll give you a note to take into Lever's medical people. So I took it in and Lever's medical people put me in touch with personnel. Personnel asked if I was in the penny in the pound, which I wasn't at the time. Well we can put you there and we'll foot the bill, we have an arrangement.

I just happened to say, well my boss was away last year, Joe Gooch, on convalescence in a big hotel in Llandudno. What's good for the goose like..... So I got put there, which was one of the top class hotels on the west shore in Llandudno. When I arrived there, I always remember, the manageress of the hotel, but before I went Lever's personnel said anything like drinks with you meal, or tea in bed in the morning or newspapers you pay for yourself. Of course, when I was leaving I asked how much I owed for the bits and pieces and she said nothing, it goes in as a bill to Lever Brothers, it won't be itemised. I said I wish you'd told me the day I arrived.

They looked after you in that respect. I couldn't knock the company as a company, but I could knock some of the younger element of management that came, known as the 'whiz kids' that started creeping in around 1968/70 - that's when it started changing, Levers.

Once when the wife and I went to a wedding in London we got salmonella and of course I struggled and drove back from London and had to get the doctor in at 7 o'clock at night when we got back and he said "How the hell you got back I don't know, with a temperature of 105." The Public Health people had to come into it then, come to your house and take samples of your motion, all that palaver. I was off work 16 weeks. But after 6 weeks I feel alright, but the Public Health people were still coming for samples of your motion and saying you can't go back. So, I contacted the bold Sister Campbell, "Can I come in and have a talk to one of the doctors?" So I goes in a sees a particular doctor and says to him "As you know I'm off work with salmonella but as far as I'm concerned I'm alright and fit enough to come back but the Public Health people won't let me come in. Do you think you could lean on somebody and get me back?" He said "Well first of all, 'lean on somebody' is a very strong sort of term. Secondly, I wouldn't have you back without clearance off the Public Health and thirdly, no way should I have you here today." Where do you go?

So after I'd been off 16 weeks and I'm going back in, this young Manager, 28 year old University lad, you know, comes up on the plant and says "Oh it's you is it?" Yorkshire man he was. I said "Who do you think it was, Father Christmas, like?" You know, chatty and that. Anyway, 10 o'clock, 'phone goes on my desk, "Can you come down to see me?" His office was downstairs. He said "I've got to tell you before I start, I've got you here on a disciplinary thing." I said "Oh aye" and I locked his door and he said "Why have you done that?" I said "Well we won't get disturbed." This was my style with these young men. I said "Go ahead, fire away son." They didn't like it , calling them son.

He said "I've been looking at your record. It's atrocious, you've just been off 16 weeks. You were off two years ago for 14 weeks with blood pressure and angina. I said "That's correct, I would agree with you." "Well I'm not having it, I'm not putting up with this." I said "Sorry but I've just been off with salmonella. It wasn't my choosing to stay off." "Well I don't care what you've been off with, I'm not having it. Top rate Chargehand, you're no good to me." I said "Look son, do what you want to do. I've been here since 6 o'clock, you come in at half-eight, I haven't eaten. Good day, do what you want to do." When I went up to my own little office I rung the Public Health people and told them the story. He said "Where do you work?" I said "Lever Brothers." He said "Can't understand it because Lever Brothers, as you've just said, have got such a good reputation."

So anyway I didn't hear any more off this Manager, didn't hear a thing. But I was telling the story about six months later to one of the Development Chemists who I had a good relationship with, clever fellows them, gentlemen. I was telling the story like I'm telling you and he said "You're not the fella are you. He got a right bollocking for trying to bring the company's name into disrepute. He got lashed. I didn't know it was you." The company was alright. It was the little Hitler's in between. The company itself, you couldn't fault it.

Another time when I had the dermatitis, one of Levers doctors implied that I was putting my hands in stuff to bring the dermatitis on, and he had a stutter this fella, and he says to me "Put your fucking cards on the table and I can put mine." The nursing sister was stood behind and she just went out in disgust because he had a reputation for his language . I just let him carry on and just sat there like a little soft lad. Then I said to him , I called him son, "First of all, I held the medical profession in high esteem until I met you. You're an animal. Don't tell me about chemicals because I was handling them before you was outside your mothers belly," I said. That's the sort of people you could get there, Levers can put a front up, but behind closed doors it was another story.

I was one of them people, before I made Chargehand, I worked 6 to 2 in my own department and I'd go to another department and do 2 till 10 and put 16 hours in. I needed the money. You could do that, to get the pennies, you know. My two eldest daughters, they went to the Wirral Grammar, once they got there they wanted uniforms, books, this and that. The money counted. I like a pint at the end of the week. If you wanted the money, you had to work like, you know.

Many a time I wanted out, especially when Vauxhalls came into the area. I nearly went there. I'm glad I never because pension-wise Levers is far superior than Vauxhalls. I couldn't really call the company. I could call some of the people that work for it, some of the management, they mis-managed people, little Hitler's. I didn't finish really on good terms. I'd been off six months as I injured my shoulder coming down a ladder. Thought I was on the bottom rung and I had one to go and I went over and caught me shoulder on an electric motor at half-past one on the Saturday, going home at 6. Sunday morning, I couldn't get me coat on. Monday I was down Levers Health Centre, X-rayed, nothing broken, nothing badly bruised. Physio for 13 weeks, going through bloody agony. Went to see my own doctor. He sent me for physio for another 13 weeks at Clatterbridge. Cutting it short - ended up eventually seeing orthopaedic, had to have the ball taken out, it was cracked and they had to clean it out. I was off six months.

I went back and was only back two days and Personnel sent for me. This is after 40 years with the company. They said "Are you wondering why we've sent for you?"

"I've got an idea you want to enquire about my health."

He said, "Partly, but the company thinks you'd be better if you went back on the sick and run your sick pay up." Because they paid you for 18 months, you see, and I'd had six of them. Then he said "We'll put you on a pension when you become 60." I was 58 and a bit when I come out.

"How do you feel about that?"

I said "Bloody indignant. Here are you sitting there; I've most probably worked longer than you've lived." He said "You have, as a matter of fact." I said "Well who are the faceless, nameless ones who say 'the company thinks'." "Oh, well I can't disclose that."

I saw the funny side because I did really want to get out, I'd had enough, you know, the way the management was changing. So I said "Well, what about my holidays from last year. If I'm going to run me sick pay up, what about next year's." They said "Don't worry about that." I said "That's alright, you said go back on the sick, but where do you propose I get sick notes?" (I'm getting round to how strong a company Levers are.) He said "Go to your doctor and he'll give one to you." I said "I don't think so." So I said "Alright. Can I go now?" He said "Yes."

So I went and emptied my locker, tied it in a bag, threw it in a skip and that's how I came out of Levers. Mind, I got a retirement party, like, you know. So I goes into me doctors, I've rung up for an appointment, goes in. Said "I've come for a sick note to stay off." Doctor said "Aren't you the fellow I gave a note last week to go back?" I said "Yes. But the company I work for has told me to stay on the sick for the next 15-18 months." He said "Where do you work?" I said "Lever Brothers." He said "Who do Levers think they are? Think I sit here willy nilly waiting for somebody to come through the door saying give us a sick note, and I just sign it?" I said "I'm not arguing with you, doctor, you get in touch with Lever Brothers."

But I got in touch with Lever Brothers and Personnel rung the doctor. I go back to the doctor and he says "Somebody's been on from Levers, it could have been one of your mates for all I know. But I'll accept it was their Personnel. How do you feel yourself about coming off on these terms?" I said "Alright." He says "Well here's a note for a month." After that ran out I went back and he said here's one for three months. When the three months was up he said "Here's one for 12 months. I'll see you when you're 60."

I finished in the February 1989, I'd been off since 1987. They'd paid me for 22 months when they hadn't any need to. But they did do.

While I was off, in January 1989, we got a good rise, a 13% rise, spread over two years and that 13% on my salary was worth £1,800 a year, so I got on to Personnel and said "What about it, like?" He said "I don't know, you've got me across a barrel there. You'll get the six weeks from the first of January to 12 February, the day you officially finish with the company." I said "Well I'm not 60 until the June. I think I should get six months." When you finish you get bits and pieces. About May, the postman had been, I opened it - from Lever Brothers - another cheque for £1,800 and another £400 ex gratia onto the lump sum because of that. I thought, well that's money I didn't expect so I had that wall built round the front of the house with it. Then about three weeks after that I got a letter off the Pension Fund, saying due to the increase in salary, your pension's gone up by £1,000 a year.

I'd do it again but I think I'd try and better myself, educate myself more than what I had done. If I knew as much then as what I know now, I could have gone a lot further, I'm sure I could. I have no real regrets about working there. No, I treated it as a game, cat and mouse with some of the management. I had a terrible run in with one just before I finished. He was notorious. He wanted to move me because of the dermatitis - the Manager, he wanted to move me on medical grounds and yet the medical profession at Levers said it was nothing I was working with and as I said to this manager, "When I went to school one and one made two but this is adding up to bloody three." So I went down and sees the head doctor, Dr. Davies ,a gentleman he was, in the Health Centre and told him the story. I said is there any reason I can't stay working up there? He said there's no reason whatsoever. You're better than you've ever been."

Anyway, the manager was adamant he was going to move me and he got it all boxed in with Personnel and the Union. So he called this meeting and had it all typed out with forms to sign. He signs it, the Union sign it and anyhow I had it about three weeks and I hadn't signed it and he come up to me when I was on 12 hour nights and he said "We haven't had the minutes of the meeting back off you." I said "No, I'm a slow reader." Just to stir him up. He said "Will you come down to the office tomorrow." So I went down and put a ring round the implications in it - if the dermatitis broke out, we still reserve the right to move you. I said I'm not having that, getting out of bed and looking at my hands to see if I've still got a job. I'm not signing that. So I signed it and put underneath it "My signature to this document does not necessarily imply that I concur with the implications thereof. I'm only signing to say I've received a copy of it."

He blew his bloody top. He said we're no further and I said "No, and I'm tired, I'm on nights. Good day." After it was all over, this guy wanted to shake hands with me and he said "In all my career" and I said "And that's not long", and he said "Nobody's ever stood up and beat me. You have. I'd like to shake your hand." I said "Just put it down as experience, son. I don't know whether to shake it or break it." That was management.

From what I hear about the place now it's terrible. It's terrible to work there, you're looking over your shoulder all the while, frightened. There's no enjoyment going to work there at all now.

When I was there, Christmas, we used to have Freddie Starr on the canteen there. Levers would organise it. Used to have a good group in the works canteen in the dinner hour. You'd go for your dinner at 12 o'clock and that would be it, like, you know. You weren't allowed out of the factory till four, but you'd go in the canteen and have a good time. Of course, when you get your presentation, your watch, that was a good night out, for 15 years. They organise turns, a good meal and plenty of booze. After your 25 years you get a month's salary, tax-free, off them. Forty years you get goods to the tune of £800. I don't think anyone gets forty years in any more. They get rid of you soon as your 50 now, I think.

The people I think about, when I started, one particular woman sticks in my mind, Ethel Smith, she'd been there since 1914. If she was still alive she'd be 95, 98. She had 46 years there, having to retire at 60. There was no pension scheme for the women. Didn't pay into one. But the firm was going to pay her 28 shillings a week after 46 years, and she worked like a Trojan, because in them days they worked, you know.

You don't have much contact with the company once you're a pensioner. You don't have any contact at all. Magazine every quarter, load of rubbish. But the pension is index-linked. To what they're coming out with now, like, my salary when I finished was £18,000 basic but the same job now carries about £25,000, you know, so it makes a difference, as you get two-thirds as pension, you see, if you've got the service in.

I think they could organise some sort of pensioners' dinner once a year. They have a pensioners' meeting once a year. Two I've been to. Didn't get a lot of information out of it. Got sandwiches but they must have been a day old because they was all curled up, you know. There's no canteen now. All meals are out of vending machines.

I was there when they was negotiating this vending machine bit. The particular job I had in No. 1 Liquids you didn't go for your break at a set time, it was where the process was up to. Sometimes it would be 4 o'clock in the morning if I was on nights before I'd get a meal. If I was going to go down to the vending machine and everyone's had their break at 2 a.m., I'd get the broken crisps, wouldn't I? When the canteen was going the meals were first class and good priced. If you worked over you always got a free meal.

You get a vast experience working in a factory. Lever Brothers employed every trade under the sun, whether they be a blacksmith, carpenter, plater, you name it. I got a lot of experience, mainly from people, oh aye. You hear stores about Cammell Lairds, stories about Vauxhall, any production line is much the same. I remember a whizz kid manager coming in saying it made no difference whether you made mars bars or packet of cigarettes, he was there to run it on a budget.

A BRIEF CHRONOLOGY OF SOAP.

1882 Lever &Co, Grocers of Bolton, register the trademark "Sunlight".

1886 Sunlight soap made in Warrington.

1888 First sod cut at Port Sunlight, Wirral.

1889 First manufacture of Sunlight soap at Port Sunlight.

1892 Company made Soapmakers to Queen Victoria.

1897 Port Sunlight weekly production is more than 2,000 tons of soap per week.

1904 Levers purchase their first motor van to deliver Sunlight soap.

1906/7 Various attacks upon company by the Daily Mail and other newspapers accusing Levers of operating an effective soap 'cartel', and giving 'short measure.' All of these attacks were sucessfully defended by the company, which won significant compensation

1908 Kings of Britain,Siam, Portugal, Spain and Sultan of Turkey grant Royal Warrants for Lever's soap.

1912 London sees performance of a show inspired by Sunlight , both the soap and the village. It was called 'The Sunshine Girl'.

1925 William Hesketh Lever, almost universally known as 'Billy Lever' dies in May.

1930 Lever Bros Ltd. merge with the Dutch Margarine -Union to become UNILEVER.

1951 The introduction to Port Sunlight of the first continous soap production system.

1984 Sunlight soap is one hundred years old.

1988 The 'model' village of Port Sunlight itself is one hundred years old.

2000 The Horizon beckons.